THE CATHOLIC LUTHER

His Early Writings

Introduced and Edited by
Philip D. W. Krey and Peter D. S. Krey

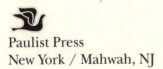

Paulist Press
New York / Mahwah, NJ

The Magnificat Put into German and Explained. From *Luther's Works*, the American edition: vol. 21 © 1956, 1984 by Concordia Publishing House. All Rights Reserved.

Sermon at the Coburg. From *Luther's Works*, vol. 51: *Sermons I*. Philadelphia, PA: Fortress Press, 1959. Used with permission.

The Sacrament of Penance, 1519. From *Luther's Works*, vol. 35: *Word and Sacrament I*. Philadelphia, PA: Fortress Press, 1960. Used with permission.

The Holy and Blessed Sacrament of Baptism, 1519. From *Luther's Works*, vol. 35: *Word and Sacrament I*. Philadelphia, PA: Fortress Press, 1960. Used with permission.

The Blessed Sacrament of the Holy and True Body of Christ and the Brotherhoods, 1519. From *Luther's Works*, vol. 35: *Word and Sacrament I*. Philadelphia, PA: Fortress Press, 1960. Used with permission.

The Confession Concerning Christ's Supper, 1528. From *Luther's Works*, vol. 37: *Word and Sacrament III*. Philadelphia, PA: Fortress Press, 1961. Used with permission.

"A Sermon on Preparing to Die," translated from "Ein Sermon von der Bereitung zum Sterben" in *Martin Luther*, ed. Johannes Schilling et al., Vol. 1: *Glaube und Leben*, ed. Dietrich Korsch (Leipzig: Evangelischer Verlagsanstalt, 2012), with permission of Evangelischer Verlagsanstalt.

Cover image: Painting by Cranach, Lucas the Elder. Photo credit: Scala / Art Resource, NY.
Cover design by Joe Gallagher
Book design by Lynn Else

Library of Congress Cataloging-in-Publication Data
Names: Luther, Martin, 1483–1546, author. | Krey, Philip D., 1950– editor.
Title: The Catholic Luther : his early writings / introduced and edited by Philip D.W. Krey and Peter D.S. Krey.
Description: New York : Paulist Press, 2016. | Includes bibliographical references.
Identifiers: LCCN 2016000688 (print) | LCCN 2016015293 (ebook) | ISBN 9780809149889 (pbk. : alk. paper) | ISBN 9781587686153 (ebook)
Subjects: LCSH: Catholic Church—Doctrines.
Classification: LCC BR331 .E5 2016 (print) | LCC BR331 (ebook) | DDC 230/.41—dc23
LC record available at https://lccn.loc.gov/2016000688

Published by Paulist Press
997 Macarthur Boulevard
Mahwah, New Jersey 07430

www.paulistpress.com

Printed and bound in the
United States of America

CONTENTS

Foreword by Dr. Wolfgang Thönissen v

Preface ix

Introduction 1

The Magnificat Put into German and Explained 23

Sermon at Coburg.. 63

The Sacrament of Penance.. 76

The Holy and Blessed Sacrament of Baptism 90

The Blessed Sacrament of the Holy and True Body of
    Christ, and the Brotherhoods 106

The Confession Concerning Christ's Supper 125

A Sermon on Preparing to Die 135

Notes 155

Bibliography 171

Index 175

FOREWORD

Wolfgang Thönissen

FOR CENTURIES, Catholics regarded Martin Luther as a heretic and the originator of a schism. At no time after the conflict of 1521 was he considered a Catholic.[1] It was first at the end of the nineteenth century that Catholic theologians began carefully to focus on Martin Luther as a person. Gradually, Catholic scholarship was able to free itself from a centuries-long, one-sided way of exploring Luther's person and work, which had become habit over the centuries.[2] Catholic interest in Reformation history, awakened through various efforts of Catholics in the Protestant-dominated German Empire, enabled Catholic theologians to formulate a basic hypothesis that claimed that Luther had overcome within himself a Catholicism that was not Catholic.[3] Joseph Lortz popularized the thesis that Luther must be described as a serious religious person and conscientious man of prayer. This picture of Luther was completed especially by Pope John Paul II, and then more recently by Pope Benedict XVI. The former stressed in 1996 that Luther's wish was to renew the Church;[4] the latter appreciated the deep passion and intensity with which Luther dedicated his entire life to the search for God.[5]

In recent times, Catholic scholarship on Luther has succeeded in clarifying the meaning of the Augsburg Confession's teaching on justification, thereby placing Luther's concerns within the broader context of the composition of the Lutheran confessions: "Thus it could be acknowledged that the intention of the Augsburg Confession was to express foundational concerns for reform and to preserve the unity of the Church."[6] Luther did not intend to split the Church. On the occasion of the four hundred and fiftieth anniversary of the publication of the Augsburg Confession, both Lutheran and Catholic theologians were able to show that the confession was not a document of division, not the foundational document of a new church, but a sign and expression of the preservation of unity in the Church.[7] In this sense, the Augsburg Confession is truly a catholic document.

Ecumenically oriented Luther research has paved the way for a proper encounter with Luther's person and theology. It brings to life a theologian and professor who was deeply embedded in medieval theology and monastic life: he concentrated his work on the interpretation of biblical literature; he appreciated and accounted for the Fathers of the Church, from Augustine to Bernard of Clairvaux; he assumed a critical stance toward Scholastic theology and Aristotelian philosophy, especially as transmitted by Scholastic theologians; and, thereby, he promoted a new kind of theology of godliness, intended primarily for laypeople.[8] In the year Luther died, Philipp Melanchthon reflected on Luther's lifetime of achievements, emphasizing that, in highlighting the "struggle for godliness," Luther summoned human thought back to Christ. Otherwise, as Melanchthon put it, Luther left the Apostles', Nicene, and Athanasian Creeds completely untouched.[9] Has it now conclusively been demonstrated that Luther was Catholic and that he remained Catholic? Did not Luther, in the course of his life, completely detach himself from his Catholicity? In the end, did not the Reformer become totally Protestant? Is the hypothesis about a Catholic Luther only something particularly for Catholics?

The writings of Martin Luther contained in this volume expressly verify the hypothesis that Martin Luther remained Catholic. However one evaluates his affiliation to the Catholic Church—as a reformed Catholic, a confessing Catholic, or even a Catholic Reformer—one can confidently fall back on Luther's own theological self-understanding. Baptism, the Eucharist, penance—for Luther they remained efficacious signs of the presence of God in Jesus Christ, incarnations of the Word of God in sacrament and preaching. Luther's rediscovery of the original gospel of Jesus Christ, under the guidance of Augustine and Bernard of Clairvaux, whom he revered as the last of the Church Fathers, did not allow him to distance himself from the sacramental and communal form of the Church. In this respect, the hypothesis of the Catholic Luther captures his fundamental conviction: the forgiveness of sins through belief in the Son of God. At the cross of Christ, the grace and mercy of God are made manifest; faith gratefully receives them. In this, Mary—"she is dear to me, the worthy maiden"—was for Luther an exemplar of faith.

Prof. Dr. Wolfgang Thönissen is Executive Director of the Johann Adam Möhler Institute for Ecumenism in the Archdiocese of Paderborn, Germany.

PREFACE

WE ARE INDEBTED to those who have introduced us to a way of being Catholic and Lutheran. We are deeply appreciative of the tradition from which Martin Luther emerged and in which he was immersed. This book is a result of our appreciation. Luther was a Catholic and had no intention to form a new church or have one named after him. In the late modern period, we have learned how traditional Luther was and that he took his place in a significant tradition of reform in the church catholic. His concern was with reforming and not reinventing medieval spirituality.[1] This reform ended in a schism in the Roman Catholic Church, which, after five hundred years, has begun to heal. Luther valued the traditional Catholic Mass and militated against those who were iconoclastic or wanted to abolish the sacraments. He had a warm Marian piety throughout his career, and although he warned against an idolatrous relationship to Mary and the saints, he valued them for their examples of faith, used them homiletically, and in prayer, considered them a part of the communion of saints.

There is no doubt that Luther also became more and more Evangelical and polemical in the course of his career, but he never abandoned the structure of his Catholic piety and he maintained a dialectical relationship with his Catholic formation—his devotional life that was so formative for him. His spiritual world was not yet emptied of Mary, the saints, and angels, as is so often the case for many of his modern followers, who, having critiqued Catholic spirituality, lack the riches of the spiritual tradition that Luther could assume and reform. Twice in his early years, Luther called upon St. Ann, Mary's mother, when he felt threatened. In the Smalcald Articles (1537), commenting on the First Article of the Creed, he describes Mary as the "pure, holy Virgin" and ends the *Commentary on the Magnificat* with the prayer: "We pray God to give us a right understanding of this Magnificat, an understanding that consists not merely in brilliant words but in glowing life in body and soul. May Christ grant us this through the intercession and for the sake of his dear Mother Mary! Amen."[2] In the sermon "On Preparing to Die," also included in this volume, he proclaims, "The apostle similarly says, 'The angels, whose numbers are legion, are all ministering spirits and are sent out for the sake of those who are to be saved' [Heb 1:14]....In addition, the person should call upon the holy angels, especially one's guardian angel, the Mother of God, all the apostles, and especially those saints whom God gave special devotion."[3]

As Roman Catholics do, Luther believed in the real presence of Christ in the Eucharist. His criticism of "sacrifice" was very focused, and one would find many Roman Catholic theologians today who would agree with his critique of how "sacrifice" was understood in his time. The differences between Luther's understanding of the Lord's Supper and that of Roman Catholics rest already in the differing theories of *how* the resurrected Christ is present, not *whether* he is present or not. In addition, in the selection in this volume, "A Sermon on Preparing to Die," Luther explains how taking the sacraments is communion with the saints:

> If the priest has given me the holy body of Christ, which is a sign and a promise of the communion

with all the angels and saints that they love me and care about me, pray, and suffer with me, die, bear sin and overcome hell, so it will be and so it must be because the divine sign will not deceive me....I would rather deny the whole world along with myself before I would doubt it. My God is certainly truthful and trustworthy for me with the divine signs and promises.[4]

This book has evolved out of our common work on the volume *Luther's Spirituality* in the Classics of Western Spirituality Series, for which we were invited to translate a number of devotional and spiritual writings by Martin Luther. In putting together that volume at the invitation of Heiko Oberman and Bernard McGinn, we were struck by how thoroughly Catholic Luther was in the structure of his spirituality,[5] or as Berndt Hamm points out, Luther is both medieval and Evangelical at the same time.[6] The ecumenical movement has brought Lutherans and Catholics into a dialogue that has included Mary, the saints, and the sacraments, which are the focus of this little volume. Although there are still differences, no issues about these teachings are truly church dividing.[7]

Thus, when our editor, Nancy de Flon, asked us to recommend a few pieces for a volume for the five hundredth anniversary of the Reformation in 2017, we were delighted to recommend Luther's *Commentary on the Magnificat* of 1521; *The Sermon at Coburg* (a sermon on St. Christopher given while the Augsburg Confession was being presented at the Diet of Augsburg in 1530); a new section on the sacraments, which treats Luther's "catholic" understanding of them as set out between 1519 and 1528; and finally his *Sermon on Preparing to Die* of 1519. Luther's Catholic devotion sustained him throughout his controversial and polemical career.

THE CATHOLIC LUTHER

The term *Catholic Luther* must always be dialectically paired with the "Evangelical" or, later, the "Protesting Luther." The Doctor of Theology was also pronounced a "heretic" by the Church of his day.[8] In an age when Lutherans and Catholics have reached agreement on the Doctrine of Justification and on many other items—except, notably, on the ministry—it is important to know that Luther's personal faith and piety, as well as his theology, contained within itself the resources for ecumenical agreement. Even his contradictory statements on Mary and the saints—some of which are included in this volume—are helpful for ecumenical dialogue because in reading them we can discover that our reconciled differences are contained in one reformer's piety. We all live with multiple religious identities and often need to construct systematic theologies to think through our own contradictions.

INTRODUCTION

AS IS TRUE of any great thinker, Luther's theologies of Mary, the saints, and the sacraments developed over the course of his career, but he always remained what Luther scholar Joseph Lortz and others have described as a "natural *homo religiosus*," that is, an ideally religious person.[1] To some degree, Luther never abandoned the devotion that shaped him as an Augustinian monk. He moved this devotion into the home via the catechisms and his personal devotion. Through the sermons, treatises, and commentaries included in this volume, he provided a resource for those in his debt, and he never abandoned a traditional focus on the proclamation of the Word and the place of the sacraments in worship. In other words, even as his Evangelical and Reformation theology developed, the layers of catholic piety that served as the foundation for his faith surfaced again and again in his writings, like rocks breaking through the plowed soil of a New England farm.[2]

MARY IN LUTHER'S PIETY

Having been nurtured in a spiritual environment that stressed the cult of Mary, it is not surprising that in 1503 the twenty-year-old law student cried out, "Mary, help!" when, on his way from Erfurt to Mansfeld, he fell and cut the artery in his leg with his dagger.[3] Two years later, frightened by a storm, he again cried out, "Help, St. Anna! I will become a monk!"[4] St. Anne was the patron saint of miners, and his father was a miner. In his volume *The Praise of Mary among the Reformers*, Walter Tappolet notes that Luther preached around eighty sermons on Mary for feast days, which give a rich picture of Luther's devotion to her. In addition, he preached on Mary as the Mother of God in Christmas sermons and many other writings, including his explanations of the second article of the Apostles' Creed and the stories of the Wedding at Cana and of the young Jesus teaching in the Temple.[5] From 1521 to his death in 1546, Luther's views on Mary did not substantially undergo development from those he presented in Magnificat, even though he later became much more critical of invoking Mary and the saints in lieu of Christ. In the Prayer Book of 1522, he accepted the Hail Mary as a "meditation in which we receive what God has given her."[6]

Luther's view of Mary evolved in the context of his work as a biblical theologian working within the intense late-medieval cult of the saints and Mary.[7] Throughout his career as a monk-priest-professor-reformer, Luther's preaching and teaching on the veneration of Mary ranged from simple piety to sophisticated polemics. His views are intimately linked to his christocentric theology and its consequences for liturgy and piety. In the Magnificat, which is included in this volume, Luther writes what could be considered a summary and centerpiece of his Marian theology and spirituality. The fact that the Magnificat is sung in Vespers, and thus influenced the liturgy, had a profound impact on Luther's spirituality. He completed the exposition during his exile at the Wartburg Castle and dedicated it to young Duke John Frederick of Saxony, who, unlike his uncle Frederick the Wise, openly supported Luther's cause. To Luther, the theme of the canticle was quite clear: Mary is the embodiment of

God's unmerited grace, and in her are contrasted true humility and the arrogance of worldly power.[8] The following passage is a fitting summary:

> "For the Mighty One has done great things for me and holy is God's name" (Luke 1:49).
>
> The "great things" are nothing less than that she became the Mother of God, in which work so many and such great good things are bestowed on her as past anyone's understanding. For on this there follows all honor, all blessedness, and her unique place in the whole of humankind, among which she has no equal, namely, that she had a child by the Father in heaven, and such a Child. She herself is unable to find a name for this work, it is too exceedingly great; all she can do is break out in the fervent cry: "They are great things," impossible to describe or define. Hence we have crowded all her glory into a single word, calling her the Mother of God. No one can say anything greater of her or to her, though we had as many tongues as there are leaves on the trees, or grass on the fields, or stars in the sky, or sand by the sea. It needs to be pondered in the heart what it means to be the Mother of God…her sole worthiness to become the Mother of God lay in her being fit and appointed for it, so that it might not take away from her God's grace, worship, and honor by ascribing too great things for her. For it is better to take away too much from her than from the grace of God. Indeed, we cannot take away too much from her, since she was created out of nothing, like all other creatures. But we can easily take away too much from God's grace, which is a precious thing to do

and not well pleasing to her. It is necessary also to keep within bounds and not to make too much of her calling her, "Queen of Heaven," which is a true enough name and yet does not make her a goddess who could grant gifts or render aid, as some suppose when they pray and flee to her rather than to God. She gives nothing, God gives all.[9]

Luther professed that Mary is the Mother of God. As he confessed in the passage cited above, the Church proclaims, "She is the *Theotokos*—the God Bearer—who brings to us the very presence of God."[10] Luther is faithful to the creeds and councils of the Church, which, especially at Ephesus in 431, proclaimed Mary the *Theotokos*. Without her, the presence of God in Jesus would not be possible. Without her, the presence of God in the Church would not be possible. Without her, the presence of God in the sacraments would not be possible. God's presence in her pregnancy does not differ from God's presence in the Lord's Supper or waters of baptism. God is present everywhere, but we find the God of promise where God has promised to be. Thereby, she fulfills the promise of the coming savior foretold by the Old Testament prophets. As we will see in Luther's sacramentology, his Christology informs how he understands Christ's presence in the sacraments and the divine presence in the Virgin Mary.[11]

Luther was also concerned that, despite all the praise that Mary deserves, she not replace Christ as the one who bestows salvific grace. He explains in his well-known treatise "On Translating: An Open Letter" why he translated the angel's greeting, "Hail Mary full of Grace the Lord is with you" (Luke 1:28), as "Thou gracious one." As Luther argued, the phrase "full of grace," would lead a German to think of her like a keg of beer, not the "gracious [*holdselige*] Mary," the "dear [*liebe*] Mary" that the angel Gabriel intended.[12] Gabriel greeted her as the Mother of God, not as one who would replace the grace of Christ whom she bore as savior: "Mary is the prototype of how God is to be 'magnified.' God is not to be 'magnified' or praised as distant, unchangeable majesty, but for unconditional, graceful, and ever-loving pursuit of God's creatures."[13] Thus Mary magnifies God for what God does rather than magnifying herself for what was done for her: "She finds herself the Mother of God, exalted above all mortals, and still remains so simple and so calm that she does not think of any poor serving maid as beneath her." This is truly "humility," "lowliness," indeed, "nothingness."[14]

As a saint, Mary is also a model of faith for Luther—the model of listening-obedience and trust. When she says, "Let it be according to your will," she demonstrates her faith in the power of the Holy Spirit to redeem the world through her child.[15] Unlike Zechariah, the father of John the Baptist, who is also greeted by an angel in Luke 1:10–20, Mary believes the angel's message. Zechariah—the priest—is struck dumb; Mary, a young woman, is a witness to who God is, and overcome by the Spirit, she proclaims God's Word. She who carries the Word of God in her womb also proclaims who that Word is in a prophetic song. She knows how to praise God. Mary also sees God as God is—a God of mercy who has done good things for her. This God shows up where one least expects: among the children of Israel, in a common and unassuming woman, and on the cross. Unlike our expectations, this God scatters the proud, lifts up the lowly, fills the hungry with good things, and sends the rich away empty. Mary is the prophet for the poor, the troubled, and all who need help. Samuel's mother, Hannah, whose prayer is an Old Testament model for the Magnificat, also proclaimed that God is an advocate for the poor, the hungry, and the lowly (1 Sam 2:1–10).[16]

Luther makes the same point in his commentary in the introduction to the Magnificat:

Even as God is called the creator and the almighty because the world was created out of nothing so also God's work continues unchanged. From now to the end of time God will make what is insignificant, despised, suffering, and dead into something valuable, honorable, blessed and alive. On the other hand, everything that is valuable, honorable, blessed, and living God will make to be nothing, worthless, despised, suffering, and dying. No creature can make something out of nothing. Therefore, God's eyes peer only into the depths, not to the heights, as Daniel says in chapter 3:55 (Vulgate): "You sit upon the cherubim and behold the depths"; in Psalm 138:6: "For though the Lord is high, he regards the lowly; but the haughty he perceives from far away." Similarly Psalm 113:5f: "Who is like our God, who sits on high and nevertheless sees below on the lowly in heaven and on earth?" Because God is the most high with nothing above, God cannot look above or alongside and since nothing is God's equal, of necessity, God must look within and below, and the farther one is below the better God sees you.[17]

Being regarded by God is the truly blessed state of Mary. She is the embodiment of God's grace, by which others can see what kind of God the Father of Jesus Christ is.[18] This is Luther's interpretation of verse 48b, "All generations will call me blessed." She does not say, Luther contends, that people will call her blessed because of her virtue, her virginity, or her humility; rather, she is blessed because God regarded her. As Timothy Wengert writes in the preface to *Luther's Spirituality*, "The theology of the cross is defined as God's revelation in

6

precisely the last place anyone would reasonably look, that is, in the gracious, faith-creating promise of the Crucified."[19]

In the Bible, wherever the Holy Spirit appears, persons begin to prophesy. Thus, as Elizabeth sees Mary's pregnancy, she is filled with the Holy Spirit and prophesies, "Blessed are you among women, and blessed is the fruit of your womb."[20] The great prophet John, in her womb, leaps for joy in anticipation. Luther sees Mary as the Mother of our Lord, as the one who ponders the great mystery that has come upon her and to humankind: that God is present deep within our existence as one of us, rejoicing with the shepherds and angels, fearful and vulnerable in the massacre of the innocents, living in companionship with family and friends, and finally suffering and dying as a victorious martyr for us. Mary ponders all these things at the beginning, with the announcement of Jesus' birth, and at the end, when grief at the death of her son pierces her heart like a sword. She is also a witness to Jesus' resurrection life, according to the Acts of the Apostles 1:14.[21] Mary is blessed of all women, according to Luther, because she knows how to rejoice, how to give thanks and praise to the God who has given her and us good things— our health, our work, our families, our homes and schools and government.

Catholic scholar George H. Tavard argues that the last sections of Luther's *Commentary on the Magnificat*, which are not included in this volume due to their length, demonstrate a twofold, threefold, and sixfold pattern similar to Bonaventure's *Itinerarium Mentis in Deum*, and that the negative theology of the whole commentary echoes the medieval German mystics, especially Suso and Tauler. Tavard points out that, for Luther, the third or unitive level in the believer's progress— the level of darkness and unknowing—is simply that of faith.[22] Tavard provides a fitting summary for the Catholic Luther's Magnificat: "In the medieval context Mary's canticle is not only biblical; it is also a liturgical hymn that is used in daily prayer. As Luther notes in dedicating the work to John Frederick, it 'is sung in all the churches at vespers, and to a particular and appropriate setting that distinguishes it from the other chants.'"[23] Tavard concludes,

> That Martin Luther in 1520–1521 practiced and recommended a certain devotion to the Mother of God is clear. This devotion was not focused on the angelic greeting, *Ave Maria*, but on Mary's hymn, Magnificat. It entailed meditating on her words and hence on Mary herself, on her life, her relation to Christ, the conditions of true discipleship, and the primacy of faith. It implied giving the Mother of God "the honor and devotion that are her due," namely, praise, imitation, and above all giving thanks to God for choosing her as the Mother of the Word made flesh. Such a devotion was squarely founded in Scripture, in the early Christological and Trinitarian dogmas, and in the nature of faith as God's gift and not a human achievement....The Virgin Mary and her song of thanksgiving stand as models of true *pietas*, a word which, in its original sense, that was still operative at the end of the Middle Ages, designated the mutual affection between parents and children. The praise of Mary is part of the Christian joy.[24]

As Lutheran scholar Eric Gritsch explains,

> Mary is the "Mother of God" who experienced God's unmerited grace. Her personal experience of this grace is an example for all humankind that the mighty God cares for the lowly just as God cares

for the exalted. That is God's work in history. Mary has no special qualifications for becoming the "Mother of God." The church, therefore, should not praise her for being worthy to bear the Son of God. She was chosen because she was a woman, just as the wood was chosen to bear Jesus on the cross. Thus she incites the faithful to trust in God's grace when they call on her. "She does nothing, God does all. We ought to call upon her that for her sake God may grant and do what we request. Thus also all other saints are to be invoked, so that the work may be in every way God's alone."[25]

THE SAINTS: LUTHER'S UNDERSTANDING OF THE COMMUNION OF SAINTS

The Christian is baptized into a cruciform way of living. To describe this baptismal calling, Luther preached a sermon titled "Cross and Suffering" in 1530, when he was in the Coburg Castle. According to the sermon, Christians must suffer; however, the cross they carry cannot be self-selected but is given to them by the devil and the world. They recognize the unsurpassed gift that Christ has become theirs in his suffering and serving. Thus Christ's suffering is so powerful that "it fills heaven and earth and tears apart the power and might of the devil, hell, death, and sin." When one's suffering and affliction is at its worst, if one thinks on Christ, then God, who is faithful, will come to help, just as God has helped God's own from the beginning of the world. To explain this, Luther invokes the story of St. Christopher, a simple story that gives an example of the Christian life and how it should be lived. When, like St. Christopher, one puts the dear Christ child on one's back, one must carry him all the way across the water or drown. In the story, as in baptism, Christopher sinks, but he clings to a tree, which is the promise that Christ will do something special with our suffering. Though it is not good to drown, Luther says, through our baptisms, we are raised again by God in Christ. In the world are trials and tribulations, but through the resurrected Christ, one has freedom. "In our drowning," says Luther, "we have the tree to which we can cling against the waves, namely, the word, and the fine, strong promises that we shall not be overwhelmed by the waves."[26]

The Sermon at the Coburg was written in 1530, when Luther was secured in the castle, and while his colleague Philipp Melanchthon and others were defending the Augsburg Confession before the Diet at Augsburg. This sermon best illustrates Luther's mature understanding of the role of the saints in the life of the Christian. He had a christocentric understanding of the human relationship with God. Christ is the only advocate for the believer in relationship to God the Father, and the saints serve as examples and role models of faith. Thus his mature understanding of the role of saints was similar to his Evangelical understanding of Mary, the Mother of God, who was not to serve as an additional mediator to Christ between believers and God. Even as he had a profound Marian piety throughout his life that was thoroughly Catholic and Evangelical at the same time, so also his devotion to the saints developed into his understanding of the communion of saints.

While Christians do not need the saints to pray or advocate for them to God the Father, nevertheless, as Luther makes clear in the explanation to the third article of the creed, we believe in the communion of saints through the power of the Holy Spirit. Thus the saints and Mary are praying in heaven with us, linking believers in communion across the ages. And even as we ask fellow members of our assemblies of communions to pray for us when we are ill or suffering in any way, so also we can ask Mary and the saints to pray for us as well, even though it is not necessary. In fact, as is true in Acts 1:14, Mary is in the center of the earliest communion of saints at prayer.[27]

The Holy Spirit links us with all the saints, both alive and dead, across the ages, together with the angels and all the company of heavenly hosts who are singing, praising, and praying to God. We ask one another to intercede for us in the earthly communion of saints; why would we not also ask the heavenly communion of saints to intercede on our behalf? This does not lessen the mediating role of the crucified and resurrected Jesus Christ, but recognizes the *koinonia* of saints, past and present, with the communion of the divine Trinity. God shows care for us, and the saints in heaven and on earth express their care for one another in prayer and mercy. Luther's contribution to the role of the saints in the spiritual life of baptized Christians was to enhance the role of living saints.

As we will see in the selections provided in this volume, Luther's world was filled with angels and demons and saints, living and dead. His world was not emptied of the supernatural, as is often the case for modern Protestants and Catholics alike. As we will see in the last work in this volume, "A Sermon on Preparing to Die," Luther notes that in order to remain in faith in the face of death, we should call upon and accept the help of the heavenly ones: the angels (especially our guardian angel), the Mother of God, all the apostles, and the beloved saints (especially the ones God has given us for special reverence).[28] Berndt Hamm comments on this passage: "Such instructions by Luther do not signify any relative weakening of Christ's mediation of salvation but signify the extension of Christology to the members of Christ who in the effective event of Golgotha could become Christ for those who need help."[29] In this sense, Luther had already extended the three images of Christ (life, grace, and salvation) to the saints.[30]

THE SACRAMENTS

Luther's theology of the sacraments developed over the course of his career. The sermons on penance and The Lord's Supper of 1519 represent a Catholic understanding of the Sacrament of Penance and transubstantiation, which still show the beginnings of an Evangelical theology's radical emphasis on faith. Nevertheless, penance remains a sacrament for Luther and he discusses the distinction between punishment and guilt in relation to its traditional parts: confession, contrition, and satisfaction. For Luther, penance consists in the Word of God or absolution; faith in this absolution; and the peace that is the forgiveness of sins that follows faith. Faith firmly believes that the absolution and the words of the priest are true and given by the power of the Holy Spirit ("Whatever you loose..." [Matt 18:18]). Luther insists that everything depends on faith, which makes the sacrament accomplish what it signifies. "This I maintain," he writes, "however, as best I can, that in the sacrament we let faith be the chief thing, the legacy through which one may attain the grace of God.[31]

One already sees in this sermon his critique of the works of satisfaction and the declaration in the first of the Ninety-Five Theses that the whole of the Christian's baptized life should be one of repentance. He argues that although contrition and satisfaction through good works should not be neglected, one can only build on the faith and trust in the sure words of Christ. Although eventually Luther only accepted two sacraments, his theology of Christ's presence allowed for multiple sacraments, and penance would have been a strong candidate, as Melanchthon argues in the Apology to the Augsburg Confession.

Eventually, like the Catholic sacraments other than baptism and The Lord's Supper, penance lacked the definitive criteria of Christ's command, word, promise, and element. Nevertheless, the sermon "The Sacrament of Penance" continues Luther's claim, already outlined in the first of Luther's Ninety-Five Theses, that the whole Christian life was to be one of repentance. Thus, as one is justified by faith and freed by the Gospel, one still finds oneself caught in sin. As a saint and sinner at the same time, the Christian lives out one's baptismal life under both the law and the gospel. Since one remains a sinner after baptism, faith in the efficacy of the sacrament to forgive is the essential part. The Christian needs to hear the words of absolution, or forgiveness, from another believer.[32]

Jane Strohl has argued that Luther's protest against the penitential system, which was rooted in indulgences, was driven by his pastoral concern. In this sermon, he is critical of indulgences, but the need for contrition and confession, as he knows them, are pastorally important. For him, the Sacrament of Penance is a comfort for troubled and terrified consciences, which would gladly be loosed from their sins and be made righteous. Finally, satisfaction is best addressed by sinning no more and doing good to the neighbor, whether enemy or friend.[33]

Baptism

In the 1519 sermon on Baptism, Luther fully endorsed the ancient practice of full immersion, as it provides a more authentic symbol of the death and new life that baptism proclaims. Candidates for baptism should be thrust completely into the water and drawn out again. He also declares that the

Sacrament of Baptism includes three things: the sign, the significance of the sign, and faith. He writes, "The significance is a blessed dying into sin and a resurrection in the grace of God so that the old person conceived and born in sin is there drowned and a new person, born in grace, comes forth and rises."[34] As noted in the Sacrament of Penance, Luther argues here too "that the whole life of the Christian is nothing else than a spiritual baptism which does not cease until death."[35] Christians "walk in their baptisms" throughout their lives.[36] Although one emerges from the water, pure sin is still present in the flesh. Therefore, one needs to remember one's baptism throughout one's life and lack of faith in baptism cancels its effectiveness: "Everything depends on faith." This analysis includes a critique of an overemphasis on the cult of the saints, as no one who is baptized is more valuable than anyone else. He also explains the vocation of the baptized according to their various roles in life, making no one more important than anyone else; that is, bishops and priests do not have a more important baptismal calling than laypersons who live out their baptismal vocations faithfully.

The Lord's Supper

In his treatise on the Lord's Supper, Luther defines *spiritual* as "nothing else than what is done in us and by us through the Spirit and faith whether the object with which we are dealing is physical or spiritual. Thus spirit consists in the use, not in the object." "Luther therefore lays down the rule that where Scripture contrasts flesh with spirit, it cannot refer to Christ's flesh, but refers to fleshliness, or the fleshly mind."[37] Luther makes these Pauline distinctions in relation to the bodily presence of Christ in the Lord's Supper, but we can see it as a pastoral affirmation for both the whole Christian body and the body politic in faith, and not a denial of the goodness of the body and its physical and psychological needs. In fact, salvation for Luther, as also in the Scripture, has both an eternal and a secular dimension. We are citizens of heaven and citizens of this world that God has created good, and thus we need to consider the health of the soul, the body, and the commonweal.

Fundamental to Luther's theology is the proclamation of the incarnation of Jesus Christ and his cross, which announces forgiveness and acceptance by our being made righteous. As Oswald Bayer notes in his recent work *Theology the Lutheran Way*, quoting Luther's treatise on the Lord's Supper of 1527, "They do not recognize the humble human form of his glory that becomes physical and that can be touched (1 John 1:1), 'But the glory of our God is precisely that for our sakes he comes down to the very depths, into human flesh, into the bread, into our mouth, and into our heart.'"[38] It is for our sake and for our salvation that the Word became flesh and dwelt among us. Thus, in our physical and spiritual needs, we cling to a God who communicates with us in the physical words of Christ's promise and illuminates us through the breaking of the bread. The good news for us then "communicated from the triune God is essentially sensory and material."[39] As we are embodied creatures, God's presence is communicated to us in forgiveness and acceptance in an embodied form. This forgiveness opens the future for salvation for health and well-being.

Thus, when in need, we hear and share with one another an embodied word for forgiveness and healing. In the face of suffering, we do not have to ask the question why, as if the hidden or naked God will reveal the mysteries of the onset of disease, mental illness, or social and structural crises.[40] God is with us in Christ Jesus and is made present in the Word proclaimed and in the sacraments made visible and tangible for us. In community, we hear a consoling word for our consciences, receive the bread and wine physically and spiritually, and live in the world out of our baptismal vocation, freed by the cross and resurrection of Christ for others. In other words, forgiveness and acceptance are carried forward and relieve stress, resentment, anger, and the need for revenge. Indeed, they lead to productivity, psychological and communal health, and well-being.

Even as by the power of the Holy Spirit, the words "This is my body; This is my blood given and shed for you..." accomplish in us what they proclaim, so also the prayer "Forgive us our sins as we forgive those who sin against us" helps us to see that God turns to us in favor. Because of this, we turn to our neighbor in mercy and acceptance. In this way, we are free to be who we are called to be and live out our baptismal calling in the world without undue anxiety. Anxiety and bodily and spiritual challenges will afflict us, and we may well need pastoral and professional help to deal with them, but we call upon God in prayer because, as Luther asserts, hope can only be proven in affliction, and thus hope makes us secure.[41] We also pray in hope because we are commanded to do so, and God has promised to listen and help. As the psalmist says, "Call upon me in the day of trouble; I will deliver you, and you shall glorify me" (50:15).

The holy sacrament of the altar, or of the holy and true body of Christ, also has three parts that it is necessary for us to know. The first is the sacrament, or sign; the second is the significance of this sacrament; and the third is the faith required with each of the first two. These three parts must be found in every sacrament. The sacrament must be external and visible, having some material form or appearance—in the case of the Lord's Supper, bread and wine. The significance must be internal and spiritual, within the spirit of the person. Faith must make both of them together operative and useful.

Introduction

The significance or benefit of the Sacrament of the Lord's Supper, according to Luther, is the fellowship or the communion of all the saints. Christ and all the saints are one spiritual body.[42] To receive this sacrament in bread and wine, then, is nothing else than to receive a sure sign of this fellowship and incorporation with Christ and all saints. He compares participating in the Eucharist to participating as a citizen in a community. It is as if citizens were given a sign, a document, or some other token to assure them that they were citizens of the city, members of that particular community. He notes that St. Paul says this very thing in 1 Cor 10:17: "We are all one bread and one body, for we all partake of one bread and of one cup." Christ takes on the sins and sufferings of the participant in the community, and the participant receives Christ's righteousness and love just as, in a community, citizens share the joys and trials of the community together. He writes, "In this sacrament, therefore a person is given through the priest a sure sign from the very God that one is thus united with Christ and his saints and has all things in common [with them], that Christ's sufferings and life are one's own, together with the lives and sufferings of all the saints."[43]

As the head of the body, Christ instituted the supper and commanded that the Christian community do this often in remembrance of what he has done, and still does, in taking on the burdens of his followers. The Christian community is also to dwell in mutual love and bear one another's burdens, but—unlike the Sacrament of Baptism, which is done once—this sacrament is to be received frequently because the tribulations of life never cease and the believer needs to be strengthened. He writes, however, "We have, therefore, two principal sacraments in the church, baptism and the bread. Baptism leads us into a new life on earth; the bread guides us through death into eternal life." Like the

17

Sacrament of Penance, this sacrament is also designed for the troubled heart, the one challenged by adversity and hungry for God. It also carries us in the hour of death from this life to the life to come. The mutual love between Christ and the communicant is expressed in the mutual love and care that members of the body share for one another, the Church, and the world around them.

Like the Sacraments of Penance and Baptism, Luther also lists faith as an essential part. He writes, "Here, now, follows the third part of the sacrament, that is, the faith on which everything depends. For it is not enough to know what the sacrament is and signifies. It is not enough that you know it is a fellowship and a gracious exchange or blending of our sin and suffering with the righteousness of Christ and his saints. You must also desire it and firmly believe that you have received it."

Luther was much more concerned with the benefits of the Sacrament of the Lord's Supper than he was about how the real presence was possible. In the Sermon of 1519, it is evident that he accepted a form of transubstantiation, but as his eucharistic theology developed, his Christology informed his understanding of real presence. As will be seen in Luther's treatise *The Confession Concerning Christ's Supper*, Luther's Christology profoundly affected his understanding of the sacraments. In fact, it could be said that the early Church's creedal understanding of "the communication of the idioms" between Christ's divine and human natures informed how Luther ultimately understood Christ to be present in the sacraments. In fact, that Mary was able to bear the Logos, or the Second Person of the Trinity, and thus participate in the life of the Trinity, and that the Church in the risen Body of the living Christ with all the saints communes and participates in the divine life through the Spirit, makes it easy for Luther to proclaim that Christ can be and is present in the water of baptism and the bread and wine of the Lord's Supper.

In his book *Mary Through the Centuries*, Jaroslav Pelikan notes that in accepting the Nicene Creed and the Definition of Chalcedon, Luther used these confessions to interpret the Scripture. His usual attribution of an appeal to Scripture alone does not apply to his theology of Mary. In addition, Pelikan points out that the Scriptures are as lean on the Trinity and the Eucharist as they are on Mary and tradition. The development of doctrine and liturgy expanded them into elaborate and magnificent liturgical and systematic theologies. As we will see, Luther's elaborate explanation of the statement "This is my body…" in the "The Confession Concerning Christ's Supper" is a far cry from these simple words.[44] In the first treatise on the Lord's Supper from 1519, it is clear that Luther still accepted transubstantiation, while in the treatise of 1528, he uses christological language to explain the presence of Christ in the elements. In either case, he is more concerned, however, with the fact of Christ's presence for the believer than he is with how he is present. Luther is also more concerned with the anti-sacramentarians of the Reformation than with the Catholic emphasis on transubstantiation. In the end, he substituted a different explanation of how Christ is present, but never yielded to the doctrine of real presence. Such presence is that of the crucified and resurrected Christ, present in the elements, present in the assembled body of the church, present in the neighbor and the world. That presence of Christ exists for forgiveness and hope, for this life and the next, for the believer's hunger and the hungering needs of the world. That presence is made real by the Word of promise addressed to the community and the individual and received in faith and trust.[45]

A SERMON ON PREPARING TO DIE

In this very pastoral writing, Luther's purpose is to help believers "not need to fear death quite so much." He is first completely practical and then tries to open our eyes to the spiritual world, where God; Christ; Mary, the Mother of God; the saints; and all the angels watch over and await us.

The practical part: be sure to write a will so that you do not leave your family and friends quarreling over your inheritance, then go, give, and receive forgiveness from those whom you have harmed and those who have harmed you as you say goodbye so that "your soul does not remain arrested in any affairs on earth." Then Luther explains why the feast day of death of the saints is called *Natale*, where they receive a new heavenly birth. Not only they, but we also receive this birth because we are all saints who are recovering sinners. Luther makes an analogy between being born from a mother's womb and the safe passage through the straight and narrow gate of death to everlasting life in Christ. God; Christ; Mary, the Mother of God; and all the saints and angels (especially one's guardian angel) watch over a dying person and provide safe passage from death to life in Christ. All are waiting for you on the other side.[46]

Luther never tires of opposing the terrifying images or pictures of death, sin, and hell with those of life, grace, and salvation provided by Christ. The dying person should focus on the life in Christ and not let the threatening pictures of death, sin, and hell come to mind. These should be contemplated in life, but they are inappropriate at death, when "death already looms large on its own account." Luther tells how Christ overcomes each of the three images for the believer.

Luther anticipates the thoughts of the dying person that steal away one's hope and lead to despair: "My sins are too great"; "I am unworthy"; "I may have received the sacrament unworthily"; or "I may be predestined not to heaven but hell!" Luther answers, "God does not give you anything because of your worthiness. God does not build the Divine Word and Sacrament upon your worthiness, but upon pure grace. God establishes you, you unworthy one, upon the Divine Word and sign [of the sacrament]."

Luther wrestles with the issue of predestination: "What if I am predestined to hell?" That is why Christ descended into hell to save you. Christ faced the image and prospect of hell when he uttered the words of dereliction on the cross, "My God, my God, why have you forsaken me?" When we gaze at the condemned savior dying on the cross, Jesus even goes as far as experiencing hell to save us from it.[47]

Luther has a way of interpreting Scripture spiritually so that the verses apply to dying, and some of his very famous sayings are in this piece; for example, "Let God be God!"; "What the true God promises and does has to be very great"; "Seek yourself not in yourself but only in Christ, and you will find yourself in him eternally"; and, "For Christ is nothing other than sheer life," and importantly he adds, "his saints just as well."

Faith in God's promises is Luther's emphasis, but the Sacrament of Holy Communion, as the sign and external Word of God, takes up most of the last *loci* or commonplaces of his sermon.[48] The sacraments "have been tried and tested by all the saints and found to be sure for all those who have faith because they have received what they indicate. We should learn to know what [the virtues of the sacrament] are, for what they serve, and how we should use them." For Luther, the sacrament brought about the communion of saints in the dying person in a very serious way: "Through the same sacrament, in addition, you become embodied and united with all the saints and enter the veritable communion of the saints, so that they die in Christ with you, bear your sin, and overcome hell." Berndt Hamm writes, "In this way, Luther integrated the late medieval concept of intercession into the *communion* idea of the body of Christ in his Reformation teaching about how to die."[49]

Sometimes Luther has been charged with fideism, so that way too much depends upon our faith. But for Luther, faith is not of our own effort or work; it is the power of God at work in us. Luther reminds us to pray that God give us that robust and staunch faith. Reminding us ever and again that God commands us to pray: "In addition the person should call upon the holy angels, especially one's guardian angel, the Mother of God, all the apostles, and especially those saints, to whom God gave special devotion. One should also pray in such a way that one not doubt that one's prayer is heard."

THE MAGNIFICAT PUT INTO GERMAN AND EXPLAINED

By Dr. Martin Luther, Augustinian

EDITORS' INTRODUCTION: *This explanation of the Magnificat was written by Luther before and after the Diet of Worms. He wrote the first third in Wittenberg at the turn of 1520/21 and the last two-thirds when he was at the Wartburg in May and June, 1521. The commentary is dedicated to the seventeen-year-old Prince John Frederick of Saxony (1503–54)[1] and serves as a mirror for princes. "Because they need not fear people," Luther comments, "rulers should fear God more than others, learning to know God and carefully to observe the works of God. As St. Paul says in Romans 12:8, 'Let the one who leads be diligent.'"*

This early commentary is also an example of Luther's Marian piety.[2] Luther considers Mary to be the Mother of God, in accordance with the tradition established by the Council of Ephesus in 431: "This holy song of the most blessed mother of God…ought indeed to be learned and kept in mind by all who would rule well and be helpful lords. The tender mother of Christ…teaches us with her words and by the example of her experience how to know, love, and praise God. With a leaping and joyful spirit she boasts and praises God for regarding her, despite her low estate and her nothingness."

George Tavard has argued that the twofold, threefold, and sixfold patterns of the commentary demonstrate the influence of Bonaventure's Itinerarium mentis in Deum, *and its negative theology echoes the medieval German mystics. For Luther, in contrast to his predecessors, the third or unitive level in the believer's progress—the level of darkness and unknowing—is simply that of faith.[3] Throughout, Luther's theology of the cross is evident. God is hidden and revealed where one would least expect to find the Almighty One, in the lowliness of a poor maiden, in suffering, in the cross.*

JESUS

To his Serene Highness, Prince John Frederick, Duke of Saxony, Landgrave of Thuringia, Margrave of Meissen, my gracious Lord and Patron.

Subservient Chaplain[4]

Dr. Martin Luther

Serene and highborn prince, gracious lord! May your Grace accept my humble prayer and service. Your Grace's kind letter has recently come into my obedient hands, and its comforting contents brought me much joy. Since I long ago promised and still owe this exposition of the Magnificat to you, since the troublesome quarrels of adversaries have so often hindered me, I decided to answer your Grace's letter with this little book. If I put it off any longer, I shall have to blush for shame, and it is not right for me to make any more excuses. I do not want to impede your Grace's youthful spirit, which inclines to the love of Sacred Scripture and would be stirred up and strengthened by more attention to it. To this end, I wish your Grace God's grace and help.

This is especially needful because the welfare of so many people depends on so great a prince, whose self-concern is removed when he is graciously governed by God. On the other hand, when he is left to himself and not governed graciously by God, many are ruined.

The Magnificat Put into German and Explained

Although all human hearts are in God's almighty hand, it is not without reason said of kings and princes, "The king's heart is...in the hand of the Lord; he turns it wherever he will."[5] In this way, God wishes to drive fear into the hearts of the great princes to teach them that they can think nothing without God's special inspiration. What other persons do brings weal or woe only to themselves or to a few people. Rulers, however, are appointed for the special purpose of being either harmful or helpful to other people. The more people, the wider their domain. Therefore, Scripture calls upright, god-fearing princes "angels of God" (1 Sam 29:9)[6] and even "gods" (Ps 82:6).[7] Conversely, harmful princes are called "lions" (Zeph 3:3), "dragons" (Jer 51:34), and "wild animals" (Ezek 14:21). These God includes among the four plagues—pestilence, famine, war, and wild animals (Ezek 14:13–19 and Rev 6–8).

Since the human heart is by nature flesh and blood, it is in itself prone to presumption. If power, riches, and honor are bestowed, it is so tempted to presumption and self-assurance that God is forgotten and subjects are neglected. Therefore, if it is at liberty to do evil without fear of punishment, it does so and becomes a beast doing whatever it wants—a prince in name, but a monster in deed. Therefore, the sage Bias has well said, "The office of ruler reveals what sort of person a ruler is."[8] As for the subjects, they do not dare to let themselves go for fear of the government. Because they need not fear people, rulers should fear God more than others, learning to know God and carefully to observe the works of God. As St. Paul says in Romans 12:8, "Let the one who leads be diligent."

Now in all of Scripture I know of nothing that serves as well for this purpose as this holy song of the most blessed Mother of God, which ought indeed to be learned and remembered by all who would rule well and be helpful lords. Here she sings most sweetly of the fear of God and of what kind of Lord God is and, above all, how God deals with those of high and low degree. Let another listen to his love singing a worldly song. This modest virgin deserves to be heard by princes and lords, as she sings her sacred, pure, and salutary song. It is also appropriate that this canticle is sung daily in all churches at Vespers and in a special and appropriate setting that sets it apart from other chants.[9]

May the tender Mother of God grant me that spirit that I may profitably and thoroughly expound her song. May God grant that your Grace and all of us may take from it a salutary understanding and praiseworthy life, so that in eternal life we may praise and sing this Magnificat. So help us God. Amen.

Herewith I commend myself to your Grace, humbly beseeching your Grace in all kindness to receive my meager attempt.

Wittenberg, March 10, 1521

THE MAGNIFICAT

My soul magnifies the Lord,
and my spirit rejoices in God, my Savior,
for he has looked with favor on the lowliness of
    his servant.
Surely, from now on all generations will call me
    blessed;
for the Mighty One has done great things for me,
and holy is his name.
His mercy is for those who fear him
from generation to generation.
He has shown strength with his arm;
he has scattered the proud in the thoughts of
    their hearts.
He has brought down the powerful from their
    thrones,
and lifted up the lowly;
he has filled the hungry with good things,
and sent the rich away empty.
He has helped his servant Israel, in remembrance
    of his mercy,
according to the promise he made to our ancestors,
to Abraham and to his descendants forever.

The Magnificat Put into German and Explained

In order properly to understand this song of praise, one must recognize that the Blessed Virgin Mary is speaking from her own experience, through which she was enlightened and instructed by the Holy Spirit, for no one can understand God or God's Word without receiving it directly from the Holy Spirit.[10] On the other hand, no one can receive it from the Holy Spirit without experiencing, proving, and feeling it. Within this experience, the Holy Spirit teaches as if in a school of the Spirit, outside of which one learns nothing but empty words and babble. Now when the Blessed Virgin herself experienced that God was working such great things in her despite her insignificance, lowliness, poverty, and despised condition, the Holy Spirit taught her this valuable insight and wisdom. God is the kind of Lord who does nothing but lower what is of high degree,[11] briefly breaking what is whole and making whole what is broken.

Just as God is called the Creator and the Almighty because the world was created out of nothing, so God's work goes on unchanged. From now to the end of time, God will make what is insignificant, despised, suffering, and dead into something valuable, honorable, blessed, and alive. On the other hand, everything that is valuable, honorable, blessed, and living, God will make to be nothing, worthless, despised, suffering, and dying. No creature can make something out of nothing.[12] Therefore, God's eyes peer only into the depths, not to the heights. As Daniel says in chapter 3:55 (Vulgate),[13] "You...look into the depths from your throne on the cherubim"; in Psalm 138:6, "For though the Lord is high, he regards the lowly; but the haughty he perceives from far away." Similarly, Psalm 113:5f., "Who is like the Lord our God, who is seated on high, who looks far down on the heavens and the earth?" Because God is most high with nothing above, God cannot look above or alongside, and since nothing is God's equal, God must necessarily look within and below, and the farther you are below, the better God sees you.

The eyes of the world and of humanity, on the other hand, look only above and want to rise above themselves. As it is said in Proverbs 30:13, "There are those—how lofty are their eyes, how high their eyelids lift!" We experience daily how all strive after that which is above them: honor, power, riches, knowledge, the good life, and everything that is lofty and great. Where such people are, everyone wants to hang around, run there, serve there gladly, be at their side, and share in their glory. Therefore, it is not without reason that the Scriptures describe so few princes and kings as faithful. On the other hand, no one wants to peer into the depths, where poverty, humiliation, want, lamentation, and fear are; from this, all avert their eyes. Where such people are, everyone runs away, flees, shuns, and leaves them alone. No one thinks to help them, stand with them, or attempt to make something out of them. So they must remain in the depths in their low and despised condition. There is no creator among humans who can make something out of nothing, although that is what St. Paul teaches, saying, "Do not be haughty, but associate with the lowly" [Rom 12:16].

Therefore, to God alone belongs the kind of seeing that looks into the depths, to need and lamentation, and is close to all who are in the depths. As St. Peter says (1 Pet 5:5), "God opposes the proud, but gives grace to the humble." For this reason, their love and praise of God flows. People cannot praise God unless they first love God. No one can love God except by knowing God as the sweetest and best. And God can only be known in this way when we are shown, feel, and experience God's works in us. Where God is thus experienced as the kind of God who looks into the depths and helps only the poor, the despised, the suffering, the lamenting, the forgotten, and those who are nothing, God is loved so fondly that one's heart runs over with joy, and leaps and dances for sheer gladness because of these gifts received. Here, then, is the Holy Spirit who can teach in just a moment such boundless knowledge and desire through experience.

Therefore, God assigns death to us all and provides, for the dearest children and Christians, the cross of Christ and countless sufferings and wants. In fact, God even lets them fall into sin in order to be able to see much and assist those in the depths, help many, perform many works, and be revealed as a true creator, dear and worthy of praise. Unfortunately, the world works tirelessly against this with eyes that overlook and hinder God's seeing, work, and help, and block our knowledge, love, and praise. [The world] thus deprives God of honor and its own joy, happiness, and salvation. For this reason, God cast the only and beloved Son into the depths of misery. Before everyone, God revealed to what end God's seeing, work, help, method, counsel, and will are directed. Thus Christ, who has most fully experienced all of this, remains eternally full of knowledge, love, and praise of God. As it is said in Psalm 21:6, "You bestow on him blessings forever; you make him glad with the joy of your presence," namely, in that he sees you and knows you. To this, Psalm 44 adds that all the saints will do nothing in heaven but praise God, because God saw them in their depths and was revealed to them as worthy of love and praise.

The tender mother of Christ does the same here, teaching us with her words and by the example of her experience how to know, love, and praise God. With a leaping and joyful spirit, she boasts and praises God for regarding her, despite her low estate and her nothingness. We must believe that she came of poor, despised, and lowly parents. To paint this for the eyes of the simple, there were undoubtedly daughters of chief priests and counselors in Jerusalem who were rich, young, educated, and held in high regard by all people, just as there are today daughters of kings, princes, and the rich. The same was also true of many another city. Even in Nazareth, her own town, she was not the daughter of one of the chief rulers, but a poor and plain citizen's daughter, whom no one looked up to or held in high regard. To her neighbors and their daughters, she was but a simple maiden, tending the cattle and doing the housework, and she was certainly no greater than any house servant who does what she is told to do around the house.

Thus Isaiah had announced (Isa 11:1–2), "A shoot shall come out from the stump of Jesse, and a branch [Luther says "flower"] shall grow out of his roots. The spirit of the Lord shall rest upon him." The stump and root is the generation of Jesse or David, in particular, the Virgin Mary; the shoot and flower is Christ. Now just as it is unforeseeable, yes, unbelievable, that from a withered, rotten stump and root a lovely shoot and flower should grow, just so unlikely was it that Mary the Virgin should become the mother of such a child. I think that she is not called the stump and root merely because she miraculously became a mother with her virginity intact—just as it is miraculous for a shoot to grow from a dead block of wood—but also because the royal stem and line of David was green and blossomed with great honor, power, wealth, and good fortune at the time of David and Solomon and was held in high regard by the world. Yet, at the time when Jesus was to come, the priests assumed this honor to themselves and ruled by themselves, and the royal line of David was as poor and despised as a dead block of wood, so that there was no longer any hope or anticipation that a king would come from it with any great glory. But when all seemed most unlikely, Christ comes, born of this despised stump, of the poor and lowly maiden. The shoot and the flower grow from a person whom Sir Annas' or Caiaphas' daughter would not have deigned to have for their humblest lady's maid.

Therefore, God's work and eyes reach into the depths, while human eyes reach only into the heights. So much for the origin of her canticle, which we shall now consider word for word.

My soul magnifies the Lord

This word is expressed with great fervor and overwhelming joy, in which her soul and life lift themselves from within in the Spirit. Therefore, she does not say, "I magnify God," but "My soul magnifies the Lord." As if she wished to say, "My life and my whole understanding soar in the love, praise, and sheer joy of God, such that I am no longer in control of myself; I am exalted, more than I exalt myself to praise the Lord." Thus it happens to all in whom godly sweetness and God's spirit has poured, that they experience more than they can describe. It is not a human work to praise God with joy. It is a joyful suffering and God's work alone and cannot be taught with words, but only by personal experience. As David says in Psalm 34:8, "Taste and see that the Lord is good; happy are those who take refuge in him." David puts tasting before seeing because this sweetness cannot be comprehended unless one has experienced it for oneself. No one attains this experience without trusting God with one's whole heart in the depths and in the distresses of life. Therefore, David adds, "Happy are those who trust the Lord." They will experience God's work and will obtain God's sensible sweetness and, through it all, understanding and knowledge.

We want to treat the words in order. The first is "my soul." Scripture divides the person into three parts.[14] St. Paul says in the last chapter of Thessalonians, "May the God of peace himself sanctify you entirely; and may your spirit and soul and body be kept sound...at the coming of our Lord Jesus Christ" [1 Thess 5:23]. Each of these three parts, as well as the whole person, is further divided into two parts, called

31

"spirit" and "flesh." This division is not of human nature but of human qualities. That is, according to nature, there are three parts—spirit, soul, and body—which can be altogether good or bad, that is, flesh or spirit, which is not now our topic. The first part, the spirit, is the highest, deepest, and noblest part of the person, through which one can attain untouchable, invisible, and eternal things. In short, it is the home of faith and God's Word. David speaks of it in Ps 51:10: "Create in me a clean heart...and...a new and right spirit," that is, a righteous and unwavering faith. On the other hand, concerning the unbelievers, he says in Ps 78:37, "Their heart was not steadfast toward [God], they were not true to his covenant."

The second part, the soul, is this same spirit, according to nature, but is seen to have the separate function of making the body alive and working through it. In the Bible, it is often spoken of as life, because the spirit can live without the body but not the body without the spirit. Even in sleep we see the soul living and working without interruption. It is its nature not to understand incomprehensible things but only that which reason can understand and consider. And it is reason that is the light in this house. Where the spirit in faith with its brighter light does not enlighten, the light of reason rules, and it is never without error. It is too inferior to deal with godly things. The Bible attributes many things to these two parts, including wisdom and understanding—wisdom to the spirit and understanding to the soul; likewise, hatred, love, delight, outrage, and the like.

The third part is the body with its members. Its work is to draw upon and apply what the soul understands and the spirit believes. To use an example from the Bible,[15] Moses built a tabernacle with three different courts. The first was the holy of holies; here God dwelt, and in it there was no light. The second was the holy place; here stood a lampstand with seven arms and seven lamps. The third was the outer court; it was open to the sky and to the sun's light. This is a metaphor for the Christian person, whose spirit is the holy of holies, God's dwelling in the darkness of faith, without light. For the Christian believes what is neither seen, nor felt, nor comprehended. The soul is the holy place with its seven lamps, that is, every form of reason,[16] discrimination, knowledge,[17] and understanding[18] of bodily and visible things. The body is the outer court that is open to everyone, so that everyone can see what one does and how one lives.

Now Paul asks the God of peace to make us holy, not in part, but entirely—through and through—so that the spirit, soul, and body may all be holy [1 Thess 5:23]. There would be much to say concerning the reasons for such a prayer, but, in brief, when the spirit is no longer holy, then nothing is holy. The greatest battles and the gravest dangers take aim at the spirit's holiness, which stands only in the pure and simple faith, because the spirit does not concern itself with tangible things, as was said. False teachers come and draw the spirit outside. One proposes this work, the other that way of becoming upright. When the spirit is not protected here and is not wise, it will come out and follow, and it comes upon the outer works and ways and thinks that it will be upright in this way. Immediately, faith is lost and the spirit is dead in God's eyes.

Then the various sects and orders arise, so that one becomes a Carthusian and another a mendicant. One tries to obtain salvation with fasting, the other with prayer; one with this work, the other with that. All of these are self-chosen works and are orders never commanded by God, but only imagined by people. They no longer hold true to faith but focus on works until they are so deep in them that they have a falling out among themselves. Everyone wants to be the best and despises the other, just as the monks of the stricter orders brag and puff themselves up. Against these holy workers and seemingly righteous teachers, Paul prays, saying that God is a God of peace and unity. Such a God these disunited and unpeaceful saints cannot have or hold, unless they let go of their own things and come together in spirit and faith that these works create only disagreement, sin, and strife and only faith makes one upright and peace-loving. As Psalm 68:6 says, "God grants us unity in the house,"[19] and Psalm 133:1, "How very good and pleasant it is when kindred live together in unity."[20]

This peace never comes unless one teaches that one is made righteous, just, and blessed not by a work or any external method, but only by faith, that is, by a firm confidence in the unseen grace of God promised to us. This I have shown at great length in my treatise, "On Good Works."[21] Where there is no faith, there must be many works, and from this follows discord and disunity, and God can no longer remain there. Therefore, Paul is not content here to say simply, "your soul" or "your spirit," etc., but "your whole spirit," for all depends on this. Here he employs a fine Greek expression, *olokleron pneuma emon*, that is, "your spirit that possesses the whole inheritance." It is as if he wished to say, "Do not be led astray by false teachings about works. The believing spirit alone possesses everything." I pray that God will protect you from the false teachings that build up works as trust in God that are, nevertheless, false assurances, because they do not build on God's promises alone. When this "spirit that possesses the whole inheritance" is preserved, both soul and body are able to remain without error and evil works. Otherwise, when the spirit is faithless, it is not possible for the soul and the whole life to be righteous and without error, even if it is filled with good intentions and opinions, and finds within its own devotion and pleasure. Therefore, because of these errors and false opinions of the soul, all the works of the body also become evil and useless, even if some fast themselves to death and do all manner of holy works. Therefore, it is important that God first protect the spirit and, after that, the soul and the body, so that we do not live and work in vain but become truly holy—not only free from visible sins, but even more from false and apparent good works.

Now, enough has been said concerning these two words, *soul* and *spirit*, as they occur frequently in the Bible. Next is the little word *Magnificat*, which means to make great, to lift up, or to hold in high regard, as in reference to one who can perform, know, and will the many great things that follow in this song of praise, such that the word *Magnificat* serves as the title of a book about the same topic. Thus, Mary shows by using this word what her canticle is about, namely, the great acts and works of God to strengthen our faith, to comfort the lowly, and to terrify those of high degree. To this threefold use and purpose of the canticle we should focus our attention and understanding, for she sang this not for herself, but for all of us, so that we would sing after her. Now, one would not normally be terrified or comforted by such great works of God, unless one not only believes that God has the ability and knowledge to do great things, but one must also believe that God wills and loves to do them. Nor is it enough that you believe God will do such things for others and not for you, thus excluding yourself, as those do who, because of their power, do not fear God and those of little courage do, who, because of their tribulations, fall into despair.

Such faith is nothing and is dead, like an illusion taken from a fairy tale. Instead, without wavering or doubt, you must imagine God's will for you, so that you trust firmly that God will and wills to do great things with you. This is a lively, active faith that pervades and changes the whole person. It forces you to fear when you are of high degree and to take comfort when you are of low degree. The higher you are, the more you must fear, and the more you are oppressed, the more you must take comfort, which is what those with a dead faith cannot do. What will you do in the hour of death? At that time, you must not only believe that God has the ability and knowledge to help you but also wants to help you. For an unspeakably great work must occur to deliver you from ever-lasting death, that you may be eternally blessed and become God's heir. To this faith, all things are possible, as Christ says (Mark 9:23). This faith alone abides. It also experiences God's works and thereby God's love, leading to godly praise and song, so that this upright person holds God in the high-est regard and truly magnifies God.

God is unchangeable. God is not made great by us in essence, but in our understanding and experience, that is, when we both lift up and esteem the grace and goodness of God. Therefore, the Holy Mother does not say, "My voice or my mouth, my hand or my thoughts," or "My reason or my will magnifies the Lord." There are many who praise God with great voice, who preach with well-chosen words, who speak much of God, who dispute, write, and paint; there are many who reason and speculate about God; moreover, there are many who lift God up with false devotion and will. By contrast, she says, "My soul magnifies the Lord," that is, my whole life and being, mind and strength esteem God highly. She is enraptured by God and feels herself lifted up into God's grace and good will, as the following verse shows.[22] In the same way, when someone does something especially good for us, our lives turn toward that person and say, "I hold that person in high regard"; in other words, "my soul magnifies that one." How much more will such a lively emo-tion be excited in us, when we experience the goodness that is so rapturously great in God's works that all our words and thoughts fall short. Our whole life should be excited, as if everything in us wants to sing praises.

But now there are two false spirits that cannot rightly

sing the Magnificat. The first are those who will not praise God unless things go well with them. As David says, "They praise you when you do good to them."[23] These persons seem to praise God, but, because they do not want to suffer oppression and be in the depths, they never experience the proper work of God and, therefore, never properly love and praise God. Thus, the world is filled with worship and praise, singing and preaching, organ and pipes. The Magnificat is sung gloriously, but it is a pity that this exquisite song should be sung by us without strength and savor, except when it goes well with us; and we do not sing it at all when things do not go well. God sinks in our estimation, and we think that God cannot or does not want to work for us, and, therefore, the Magnificat must also be left out.

The others are even more dangerous. They err on the other side. They exalt themselves because of the gifts God has given them and do not attribute them to God alone. They want credit for them. They want to be honored for them and to be considered more worthy than others. They consider all the good things that God has done for them and cling to them, claiming them as their own doing and regarding themselves as better than those who have no such things. This is certainly a slippery stance. God's good gifts naturally produce proud and complacent hearts. Therefore, we must heed Mary's last word, "God." Mary does not say, "My soul makes itself great," or "holds me in high regard." She thought nothing of herself. God alone makes her great. She credits God with everything and gives all the glory to God, from whom she has received it. Although she experienced such a great work of God within herself, she did not consider herself greater than even the lowliest person on earth. Had she done this, she would have fallen with Lucifer into the depths of Hell.

She had no thought but this: if any other young woman had received such good things from God, she would be just as glad and would not grudge them to her; indeed, she regarded herself alone as unworthy of such honor and all others as worthy of it. She would have been content had God withdrawn these blessings from her and bestowed them upon another before her very eyes. So little did she lay claim to anything, but left all of God's gifts freely in God's hands, being herself no more than a cheerful guest chamber and willing hostess to so great a Guest. Therefore, she also kept all these things forever, that is, to magnify God alone, to count only God great and lay claim to nothing. We see here how strong an incentive she had to fall into sin, so that it is no less a miracle that she refrained from pride and arrogance than that she received the gifts she did. Tell me, was not hers a wondrous soul? She finds herself the mother of God, exalted above all mortals, and still remains so simple and so calm that she does not think of any poor serving maid as beneath her. Oh, we poor mortals! If we come into a little wealth or might or honor, or even if we are a little prettier than others, we cannot abide being made equal to anyone beneath us, but are puffed up beyond all measure. What should we do if we possessed such great and lofty blessings?

Therefore, God lets us remain poor and hapless, because we cannot leave God's tender gifts undefiled or keep an even mind, but let our spirits rise or fall according to how God gives or takes away God's gifts. But Mary's heart remains the same at all times: she lets God have God's will with her and draws from it only a good comfort, joy, and trust in God. This we too should do, that would be to sing a right Magnificat.

And my spirit rejoices in God my Savior.

We have seen what is meant by "spirit"; it is that which lays hold by faith on things incomprehensible. Mary, therefore, calls God her Savior, or her Salvation, even though she neither saw nor felt that this was so, but trusted in sure confidence that God was her Savior and her Salvation. This faith came to her through the work God had done within her. And truly, she sets things in their proper order when she calls God her Lord before calling God her Savior, and when she calls God her savior before recounting God's works. In this way, she teaches us to love and praise God for God's very self alone, and in the right order, and not selfishly to seek anything at God's hands.[24] This is done when one praises God because God is good, regards only God's bare goodness, and finds one's joy and pleasure in that alone. That is a lofty, pure, and tender mode of loving and praising God and well becomes this Virgin's high and tender spirit.

But the impure and perverted lovers, who are nothing else than parasites and who seek their own advantage in God, neither love nor praise God's bare goodness, but have an eye to themselves and consider only how good God is to them, that is, how deeply God makes them feel God's goodness and how many good things God gives to them. They esteem God highly, are filled with joy, and sing God's praises, so long as this feeling continues. But just as soon as God hides God's face and withdraws the rays of divine goodness, leaving them bare and in misery, their love and praise are at an end. They are unable to love and praise the bare, unfelt goodness that is hidden in God. By this, they prove that their spirit did not rejoice in God, their Savior, and that they had not true love and praise for God's bare goodness. They delighted in their salvation much more than in their Savior, in the gift more than in the Giver, in the creature rather than in the Creator. For they are not able to preserve an even mind in plenty and in want, in wealth and in poverty. As St. Paul says (Phil. 4:12): "I know what it is to have little, and I know what it is to have plenty."

Here the words of Psalm 49:18 apply: "They will praise you when you do well with them."[25] That is to say, "They do not love you by themselves, if they have but your good and pleasant things, they do not care for you." As Christ also said to those who sought him (John 6:26): "Very truly, I tell you, you are looking for me, not because you saw signs, but because you ate your fill of the loaves...."

Now, it is much more difficult to practice moderation in riches, honor, and power than in poverty, dishonor, and weakness, since the former are mighty incentives to evildoing. So the wondrous pure spirit of Mary is worthy of even greater praise, because having such overwhelming honors heaped upon her head, she does not let them tempt her, but acts as though she did not see it, remains "even and right in the way," clings only to God's goodness, which she neither sees nor feels, overlooks the good things she does feel, and neither takes pleasure nor seeks her own enjoyment in it. In this way, she can truly sing, "My spirit rejoices in God, my Savior." It is indeed a spirit that exults only in faith and rejoices not in the good things of God that she felt, but only in God, whom she did not feel and who is her Salvation, known by her in faith alone. Such are the truly lowly, naked, hungry, and God-fearing spirits, as we shall see below....[26]

> *For God has regarded the low estate of his handmaiden.*
> *For behold, henceforth all generations will call me*
> *blessed.*

The word "low estate" has been translated "humility" by some, as though the Virgin Mary referred to her humility and boasted of it; hence, certain prelates also call themselves *humiles*. But that is very wide of the mark, for no one can boast of any good thing in the sight of God without sin and perdition. In God's sight, we ought to boast only of God's pure grace and goodness, which is bestowed upon us unworthy ones, so that not our love and praise but God's alone may dwell in us and preserve us. Thus, Solomon teaches us [what] to do (Prov 25:6–7), "Do not put yourself in the king's presence or stand (that is pretend to be something) in the place of the great; for it is better to be told, 'Come up here,' than to be put lower in the presence of the prince." How should such pride and vainglory be attributed to this pure and righteous Virgin, as though she boasted of her humility in the presence of God? For humility is the highest of all the virtues and no one could boast of possessing it except the very proudest of mortals. It is God alone who knows humility; God alone brings it to light; so that no one knows less about humility than the one who is truly humble.

In Scriptural usage, "to humble" means "to bring down," or "to bring to nothing." Hence, in Scriptures, Christians are frequently called poor, afflicted, despised. In this way in Psalm 116:10, "I am greatly afflicted"—that is humbled. Humility, therefore, is nothing else than a disregarded, despised, and lowly estate, such as that of persons who are poor, sick, hungry, thirsty, in prison, suffering, and dying. Such was Job in his afflictions, David when he was thrust out of his kingdom, and Christ as well as all Christians in their distresses. Those are the depths of which we said above that God's eyes look only into them, but human eyes only to the heights, namely, to that which is splendid and glorious and makes a brave demonstration. Therefore, in the Scriptures (Zech 12:4), Jerusalem is called a city upon which God's eyes are open—that is to say, Christendom lies in the depths and is despised by the world; therefore, God regards her, and God's eyes are always fixed upon her, as it says in Psalm 32:8: "I will counsel you with my eye upon you."

St. Paul also says in 1 Corinthians 1:27–28: "God chose what is foolish in the world to shame the wise. God chose what is weak in the world to shame the strong. God chose what is low and despised in the world, even things that are not, to bring to nothing things that are." In this way, God turns the world with all its wisdom and power into foolishness and gives us another wisdom and power. Since, then, it is God's manner to regard things that are in the depths and disregarded, I have rendered the word "humility" with "nothingness" or "low estate." This, therefore, is what Mary means: God has regarded me, a poor, despised, and lowly maiden, though God might have found a rich, renowned, noble, and mighty queen, the daughter of princes and great lords. God might have found the daughter of Annas or of Caiaphas, who held the highest position in the land. But God's pure and gracious eyes fell on me and used so poor and despised a maiden, in order that no one might glory in God's presence, as though one were worthy of this, and that I must acknowledge it all to be pure grace and goodness, and not at all my merit or worthiness."

Now, we described above at length how lowly was the estate of this tender Virgin and how unexpectedly this honor came to her, that God should regard her with such abundant grace. Hence, she does not glory in her worthiness nor yet in her unworthiness, but solely in the divine regard, which is so exceedingly good and gracious that God deigned to look upon such a lowly maiden, and to look upon in so glorious and honorable a fashion. They, therefore, do her an injustice who hold that she gloried neither in the one nor in the other, but only in the gracious regard of God. Hence, the stress lies not on the word "low estate," but on the word "regarded." For not her humility but God's regard is to be praised. When a prince takes a poor beggar by the hand, it is not the beggars' lowliness but the prince's grace and goodness that is to be commended....

The truly humble look not to the result of humility but, with a simple heart, regard things of low degree and gladly associate with them. It never once enters their mind that they are humble. Here the water flows from the well; here it follows naturally and as a matter of course, that they will cultivate humble conduct, humble words, places, faces, and clothing, and shun as far as possible great and lofty things. Thus David says in Psalm 131:1: "O Lord, my heart is not lifted up, my eyes are not raised too high." And Job 22:29 says: "The one who has been humbled shall be in glory; and the one whose eyes are bowed down shall be saved." In this way, honors always come unexpectedly upon them, and their exaltation is a surprise to them; for they have been simply content with their lowly station and never aspired to the heights. But the falsely humble wonder why their glory and honor are so long in coming: their secret, false pride is not content with their low estate but aspires in secret ever higher and higher.

True humility, therefore, never knows that it is humble, as I have said, for if it knew this, it would turn proud from contemplation of so fine a virtue. But it clings with all its heart and mind and senses to lowly things, sets them continually before its eyes, and ponders them in its thoughts. And because it sets them before its eyes, it cannot see itself not become aware of itself, much less of lofty things. And therefore, when honor and elevation come, they must take it unawares and find it immersed in thoughts of other things. Thus Luke tells us (Luke 1:29) that Mary was troubled at the angel's saying and considered in her mind what sort of greeting this might be, since she had never expected anything like it. Had it come to Caiaphas' daughter she would have not considered in her mind what sort of greeting it was, but would have accepted it immediately, thinking: "Oh how wonderful! This is just as it should be."

False humility, on the other hand, never knows that it is proud; for if it knew this, it would soon grow humble from contemplation of that ugly vice. But it clings with heart and mind and senses to lofty things, sets them continually before its eyes, and ponders them in its thoughts. And because it does this, it cannot see itself nor become aware of itself. Hence, honors come to it not unawares or unexpectedly, but find it immersed in thoughts of them. But dishonor and humiliation take it unawares and when it is thinking of something far different.

It is in vain, therefore, to teach persons to be humble by teaching them to set their eyes on lowly things, nor does anyone become proud by setting one's eyes on lofty things. Not the things but our eyes must be changed; for we must spend our life here in the middle of things both lowly and lofty. It is our eye that must be torn out, as Christ says.[27] Moses does not tell us (Gen 3:7) that Adam and Eve saw different things after the Fall, but he says that their eyes were opened and they saw that they were naked, though they had been naked before and were not aware of it. Queen Esther wore a precious crown upon her head, yet she said it seemed but a filthy rag in her eyes (Esth 14:16). The lofty things were not removed out of her sight, but being a mighty queen, she had them before her in great abundance, and not a lowly thing within sight: yet her eyes were humble, her heart and mind did not look at the lofty things, and thus God accomplished wondrous things through her. It is thus not the things but we that must be changed in heart and mind. Then we shall know of ourselves how to despise and shun lofty things and how to esteem and work and seek after lowly things. Then humility is truly good and steadfast in every way, and yet is never aware that it is humble. All things are done gladly, and the heart is undisturbed, however things may shift and turn, from high to low, from great to small.

Oh, much pride lurks behind that humble garb, speech, and conduct, of which the world is so full today. People despise themselves, yet so as to be despised by no one else; they fly from honors, yet so as to be pursued by honors; they shun lofty things, but in order to be esteemed and praised, and yet not have to have their lowly things accounted all too low. But this holy virgin points to nothing except her low estate. In it she was content to spend the remainder of her days, never seeking to be honored or exalted or ever becoming aware of her own humility. For humility is so tender and precious a thing that it cannot abide beholding its own face; that belongs to God's eyes alone, as it is said in Psalm 113:6: "God looks far down upon the lowly in the heavens and on earth." For if anyone could see one's humility, one could judge oneself worthy of salvation, and thus anticipate God's judgment; for we know that God certainly saves the humble. Therefore, God must reserve to God's very self the right to know and look at humility and must hide it from us by setting before our eyes things of low degree and exercising us in them so that we may forget to look at ourselves. That is the purpose of the many sufferings, of death, and all manner of afflictions we have to bear on earth; by means of the trouble and pain they cause us, we are to tear out the evil eye.

Thus the word "low estate" shows us plainly that the Virgin Mary was a poor, despised, and lowly maiden, who served God in her low estate, nor knew it was so highly esteemed by God. This should comfort us and teach us that though we should willingly be humbled and despised, we ought not to despair as though God were angry at us. Rather, we should set our hope on God's grace, concerned only lest we be not cheerful and contented enough in our low estate and lest our evil eye be opened too wide and deceive us by secretly lusting after lofty things and satisfaction with self, which is the death of humility. What profit is it to the damned that they are humbled to the lowest degree, since they are not willing and content to be where they are? Again, what harm is it to all angels that they are exalted to the highest degree, so long as they do not cling to their station with false desire? In short, this verse teaches us to know God aright, because it shows us that God regards the lowly, as we have said above. From such knowledge flows love and trust in God, by which we yield ourselves and gladly obey God.

As Jeremiah says (Jer 9:23–24): "Do not let the wise boast in their wisdom, do not let the mighty boast in their might..., but let those who boast boast in this, that they understand and know me, that I am the Lord." And St. Paul teaches (2 Cor 10:17): "Let the one who boasts, boast in the Lord." Now, after lauding her God and Savior with pure and single spirit, and after truly singing the praises of God's goodness by not boasting of God's gifts, the Mother of God addresses herself in the next place to the praise also of God's works and gifts. For, as we have seen, we must not fall upon the good gifts of God or boast of them, but make our way through them and ascend to God, cling to God alone, and highly esteem God's goodness. Thereupon, we should praise God and also God's works, in which are shown God's goodness for our love, trust, and praise. In this way, God's works are simply that many incentives to love and praise God's bare goodness that rules over us.

Mary begins with herself and sings what God has done for her. In this way, she teaches us a twofold lesson. First, every one of us should pay attention to what God does for one rather than to all the works God does for others. For no one will be saved by what God does to another, but only by what God does to you. When St. Peter asked about John (John 21:21): "What about this man?" Christ answered him by saying (John 21:22); "What is that to you? Follow me." But now the world is captive to a dreadful abuse—the sale and distribution of good works—by which certain audacious spirits would assist others, especially such as live or die without good works of their own, just as if these spirits had a surplus of good works. But St. Paul plainly says in 1 Corinthians 3:8: "Each will receive wages according to the labor of each"— certainly not according to that of anyone else.

It would be tolerable if they prayed for others, or brought their works before God by way of intercession. But since they deal with their works as if they were something they had to give away, it becomes a scandalous piece of business. And worst of all, they give away works of theirs of whose value in God's sight they themselves are ignorant, for God looks not at the works but at the heart and at the faith by which God works with us. To this they pay not the least attention, but trust only on the external works, deceiving themselves and all others besides. They have even gone so far as to persuade men to don the monk's cowl on their deathbeds, pretending that whatever dies in that sacred habit receives indulgence for all his sins and is saved. In this way, they have begun to save people not only with the works but with the clothes of others. Unless we see to it, I fear the evil spirit will drive them on to bring to heaven by means of monastic diet, cells, and burial. Great God, what gross darkness is this! A monk's cowl makes a man pious and saves him! Where, then, is the need of faith? Let us all turn monk or all die in cowls! At this rate, all the cloth would go to the making of monk's cowls. Beware, beware of wolves in such sheep's clothing; they will deceive you and tear you limb from limb. Remember that God works in you, and base your salvation on no other works than those God works in you alone, as you see the Virgin Mary do here. To let the intercession of others assist you in this is right and proper; we ought all to pray and work for one another. But no one should depend on the works of others, without the works of God in oneself. Everyone should make an effort to regard oneself and God as though God and that one were the only persons in heaven and on earth, and as though God were dealing with no one else than with oneself. Only then may one glance at the works of others.

In the second place, she teaches us that everyone should strive to be foremost in praising God by demonstrating the works God has done for one, and by praising God for the works that have been done to others. Thus, we read (Acts 15:2) that Paul and Barnabas declared to the apostles the works God had done by them, and that the apostles in turn rehearsed those God had done by them. The same was done by the apostles, in Luke 24:34–35, with respect to the appearances of Christ after his resurrection. There arose a common rejoicing and praising of God, each one praising the grace bestowed on another, yet most of all that bestowed on himself, however much more modest it was than that of the other. So simple-hearted were they that all desired to be foremost, not in possessing the gifts but in praising and loving God; for God's very self and God's bare goodness were sufficient for them, however small God's gifts. But the hirelings and mercenaries grow green with envy when they observe that they are not the first and foremost in possessing the good things of God; instead of praising, they murmur because they are made equal to or lower than others, like the laborers in the Gospel (Matt 20:11–12) who murmured against the householder, not because he did them any wrong, but because he made them equal to the other laborers by giving to all the same pay.

Even so we find people today who do not praise the goodness of God because they cannot see that they have received the same things as St. Peter or any other of the saints, or as this or that person living on earth. They imagine they also would praise and love God if they possessed as much as these, and they despise the good gifts of God which are showered so abundantly upon them and which they altogether

48

overlook—such as life, body, reason, goods, honor, friends, the ministration of the sun, and all created things. And even if they had all the good things of Mary, they still would not recognize God in them or praise God because of them. For as Christ says in Luke 16:10: "Whoever is faithful in a very little is also faithful in much; and whoever is dishonest in a very little is dishonest also in much." Therefore, because they despise the little and the few things, they are not worthy of the much and the great things. But if they praised God in the little, the much would also be added to them. They act as they do because they look above them and not beneath them; if they looked beneath them, they would find many that have not half of what they have and yet are content in God and sing God's praise. A bird pipes its lay and is happy in the gifts it has, nor does it murmur because it lacks the gift of speech. A dog frisks joyfully about and is content, even though it is without the gift of reason. All animals live in contentment and serve God in love and praise. Only the evil, villainous eye of a human is never satisfied, nor can it ever be really satisfied because of its ingratitude and pride. It always wants the best place at the feast as the chief priest (Luke 14:8); it is not willing to honor God, but would rather be honored by God.

There is a tale dating back to the days of the Council of Constance, of two cardinals who were riding around when they spied a shepherd standing in a field and weeping. One of the two cardinals, being a good soul and unwilling to pass by without offering the man some comfort, rode up to him and asked him why he wept. The shepherd, who was weeping bitterly, was a long time replying to the cardinal's question. At last, pointing his finger at a toad, he said: "I weep because God has made me so well favored a creature, and not hideous like this reptile, and I have never yet acknowledged it or thanked and praised God for it." The cardinal beat his breast and trembled so violently that he fell from his mount. He had to be carried to his lodging and he cried out, "O St. Augustine, how truly you have said: 'The unlearned start up and take heaven by violence, and we with all our learning, look how we wallow in flesh and blood.'"[28] Now I am sure that this shepherd was neither rich nor handsome nor powerful; nevertheless, he had so clear an insight into God's good gifts and pondered them so deeply that in them he found more than he could comprehend.

Mary confesses that the highest work that God did for her was to look upon her with favor, which is indeed the greatest of God's works, on which all the rest depend and from which they all derive. For where it comes to pass that God turns God's face toward one to favor one, there is nothing but grace and salvation, and all the gifts and works must follow. Thus we read in Genesis 4:4–5 that God had regard for Abel and his offering, but for Cain and his offering God had no regard. Here is the origin of many prayers in the Psalter—that God would lift up God's countenance upon us, "Do not hide your face from me," and "Let the light of your face shine on us, O Lord."[29] And that Mary regards this as the chief thing, she indicates by saying: "Behold, since God has regarded me, all generations will call me blessed."

Not that she does not say people will speak all manner of good of her, praise her virtues, exalt her virginity or her humility, or sing of what she has done. But for this one thing alone, that God looked with favor upon her, all generations will call her blessed, that is, to give all the glory to God as completely as it can be done. Therefore, she points to God's favor and says: "Surely, from now on all generations will call me blessed." She is not praised by God's grace toward her. In fact, she is despised, and she despises herself in that she says her low estate was regarded by God. Therefore, she also mentions her blessedness before enumerating the works that

God did to her, and ascribes it all to the fact that God looked with favor on her low estate.

From this we may learn how to show her the honor and devotion that are her due. How ought one to address her? Keep these words in mind, and they will teach you to say: "O Blessed Virgin, Mother of God, you were nothing and all despised; yet God in God's grace looked with favor on you and worked such great things in you. You were worthy of none of them, but the rich and abundant grace of God was upon you, far above any merit of yours. Hail to you! Blessed are you now and forever in finding such a God." You need not fear that she will take it amiss if we call her unworthy of such grace. For, of truth, she did not lie when she herself acknowledged her unworthiness and nothingness, which God regarded not because of any merit in her, but solely by grace.

But she does take it amiss that the vain chatterers preach and write so many things about her merits. They are set on proving their own skill and fail to see how they spoil the Magnificat, make the Mother of God, a liar, and diminish the grace of God. For, in proportion as we ascribe merit and worthiness to her, we lower the grace of God and diminish the truth of the Magnificat. The angel salutes her only as highly favored of God, and because the Lord is with her (Luke 1:28), which is why she is blessed among women. In this way, all those who heap such great praise and honor upon her head are not far from making an idol of her, as though she were concerned that people should honor her and look to her for good things, when in truth she thrusts this from her and would have us honor God in her and come through her to a good confidence in God's grace.

Whoever, therefore, would show her the proper honor must not regard her alone and by herself, but set her in the presence of God and far beneath, must there strip her of all honor, and regard her low estate, as she says; he should then marvel at the exceedingly abundant grace of God, who regards, embraces, and blesses so poor and despised a mortal. Thus, regarding her, you will be moved to love and praise God for God's grace, and drawn to look for all good things to God, who does not reject but graciously regards poor and despised and lowly mortals. Thus your heart will be strengthened in truth and love and hope. What do you suppose would please her more than to have you come through her to God this way, and learn from her to put your hope and trust in God, notwithstanding your despised and lowly estate, in life as well as in death? She does not want you to come to her, but through her to God.

Again, nothing would please her better than to have you turn in fear from all lofty things on which people set their hearts, seeing that, even in his mother, God neither found nor desired anything of high degree. But the masters who so depict and portray the blessed Virgin that there is found in her nothing to be despised, but only great and lofty things—what are they doing but contrasting us with her, instead of her with God? In this way, they make us timid and afraid and hide the Virgin's comfortable picture, as the images are covered over in Lent. For they deprive us of her example, from which we might take comfort; they make an exception of her and set above all examples. But she should be, and herself gladly would be, the foremost example of the grace of God, to incite all the world to trust in this grace and to love and praise it, so that through her, the hearts of all should be filled with such knowledge of God that they might confidently say: "O Blessed Virgin, Mother of God, what great comfort God has shown us in you, by so graciously regarding your unworthiness and low estate. This encourages us to believe that henceforth God will not despise his poor and lowly ones, but graciously regard us also, according to your example."

The Magnificat Put into German and Explained

What do you think? David, St. Peter, St. Mary Magdalene, and the like are examples to strengthen our trust in God and our faith, by reason of the great grace bestowed on them without their worthiness, for the comforting of all people. Will not the blessed Mother of God also gladly be such an example to all the world? But now she cannot be this because of the overenthusiastic eulogists and the empty chatterers, who do not show the people from this verse how the exceeding riches of God joined in her with her utter poverty, the divine honor with her low estate, the divine glory with her shame, the divine greatness with her smallness, the divine goodness with her lack of merit, the divine grace with her unworthiness. On this basis, our love and affection toward God would grow and increase with all confidence, which is why her life and works, as well as the lives and works of all the saints, have been recorded. But now we find those who come to her for help and comfort, as though she were a divine being, so that I fear there is now more idolatry in the world than ever before....

For The Mighty One has done great things for me, and God's name is holy.

Here she sings in one breath of all the works that God has done for her and observes the proper order. In the preceding verse, she sang of God's favor and gracious good will toward her, which is indeed the greatest and chief work of grace, as we have said. Now she comes to the works and gifts. For God indeed gives to some many good things and richly adorns them, as were given to Lucifer in heaven. God scatters and broadcasts gifts among the multitude, but does not therefore favor them. These good things are merely gifts, which last for a season; but God's grace and favor are the inheritance, which lasts forever, as St. Paul says in Romans

6:23: "The grace of God is eternal life." In giving us the gifts, God gives only what belongs to God, but in God's grace and favor on us, we are given God's very self. In the gifts, we touch God's hand, but in God's gracious favor, we receive God's heart, spirit, mind, and will. In this way, the blessed Virgin puts God's favor in the first and highest place, and does not begin by saying: "All generations will call me blessed, because God has done great things for me," as this verse says; but she begins: "God has looked with favor on my lowliness," as the preceding verse shows. Where God's gracious will is, there also are God's gifts; but on the other hand, God's gracious will is not also where the gifts are. This verse logically follows the preceding verse. We read in Genesis 25:5–6 that Abraham gave gifts to the sons of his concubines; but to Isaac, his natural son by his true helper Sarah, he gave the whole inheritance. Thus God would not have the true children put their trust in goods and gifts, spiritual or temporal, however great they be, but in God's grace and very self, yet without despising the gifts.

Nor does Mary enumerate any good things in particular, but gathers them all together in one word and says, "The Mighty One has done great things for me." That is: "Everything God has done for me is great." She teaches us here that the greater devotion there is in the heart, the fewer words are uttered. For she feels that however she may strive and try, she cannot express it in words. Therefore, these few words of the Spirit are so great and profound that no one can comprehend them without having, at least in part, the same Spirit. But for the unspiritual, who deal in many words and much loud noise, such words seem utterly inadequate and wholly without salt or savor. Christ also teaches us in Matthew 6:7 not to speak much when we pray, as the unbelievers do, for they think that they will be heard for their many words. Even so, there is today in the churches a great ringing of the bells, blowing of trumpets, singing, shouting, and intoning, yet I fear precious little worship of God, who wants to be worshipped in spirit and truth, as he says in John 4:24....

The "great things" are nothing less than that she became the Mother of God, in which work so many and such great good things are bestowed on her as past anyone's understanding. For on this there follows all honor, all blessedness, and her unique place in the whole of humankind, among which she has no equal, namely, that she had a child by the Father in heaven, and such a Child. She herself is unable to find a name for this work, it is too exceedingly great; all she can do is break out in the fervent cry: "They are great things," impossible to describe or define. Hence we have crowded all her glory into a single word, calling her the Mother of God. No one can say anything greater of her or to her, though we had as many tongues as there are leaves on the trees, or grass on the fields, or stars in the sky, or sand by the sea. It needs to be pondered in the heart what it means to be the Mother of God.[30]

Mary also freely ascribes all to God's grace, not to her merit. For though she was without sin, yet that grace was far too great for her to deserve it in any way. How should a creature deserve to become the Mother of God? Though certain scribblers make much ado about her worthiness for such motherhood, I prefer to believe her rather than them. She says her lowliness was regarded by God, not to reward her for anything she had done, but "The Mighty One has done great things for me." God has done this willingly without any doing of mine. Never in all her life did she think to become the Mother of God, still less did she prepare or make herself suitable for it. The greeting took her by surprise, as Luke reports (Luke 1:29). Merit, however, is not unprepared for its reward, but deliberately seeks and awaits it.

It is no valid argument against this to cite the words of the hymn "*Regina coeli laetare*": "For he whom you merit to bear" and, again, "Who you were worthy to bear." For the same things are sung about the holy cross, which was a thing of wood and incapable of merit. The words are to be understood in this sense: in order to become the Mother of God, she had to be a woman, a virgin, of the tribe of Judah, and had to believe the angelic message in order to become worthy, as the Scriptures foretold. As the wood had no other merit or worthiness than that it was suited to be made into a cross and was appointed by God for that purpose, so her sole worthiness to become the Mother of God lay in her being fit and appointed for it, so that it might not take away from her God's grace, worship, and honor by ascribing too great things for her. For it is better to take away too much from her than from the grace of God. Indeed, we cannot take away too much from her, since she was created out of nothing, like all other creatures. But we can easily take away too much from God's grace, which is a precious thing to do and not well pleasing to her. It is necessary also to keep within bounds and not to make too much of her, calling her "Queen of Heaven," which is a true enough name and yet does not make her a goddess who could grant gifts or render aid, as some suppose when they pray and flee to her rather than to God. She gives nothing; God gives all, as we see in the words that follow.

"The Mighty One," truly, in these words she takes away all might and power from every creature and bestows them on God alone. What great boldness and robbery on the part of so young and tender a maiden! She dares by this one word, to make all the strong feeble, all the mighty weak, all the wise foolish, all the famous despised, and God alone the Possessor of all strength, wisdom, and glory. For this is the meaning of the phrase: "The Mighty One." There is none that does anything, but as St. Paul says in Ephesians 1: "God accomplishes all in all."[31] And all creatures' works are God's works. Even as we confess in the Creed: "I believe in God the Father almighty." God is almighty because it is God's power alone that works in all and through all and over all. Thus, St. Anna, the mother of Samuel, sings in 1 Samuel 2:9: "Not by might does one prevail." St. Paul says in 2 Corinthians 3:5: "Not that we are competent of ourselves to claim anything as coming from us: our competence is from God." This is a most important article of faith, including many things; it completely puts down all pride, arrogance, blasphemy, fame, and false trust, and exalts God alone. It points out the reason why God alone is to be exalted—because God does all things. This is easily said but hard to believe and to translate into life. For those who carry it out in their lives are most peaceable, composed, and simple-hearted folk, who lay no claim to anything, knowing well it is not theirs but God's.

This then, is the meaning of these words of the Mother of God: "In all those great and good things, there is nothing of mine, but God, who alone does all things and whose power works in all, has done such great things for me." For the word "mighty" does not denote a quiescent power, as one says of a temporal king that he is mighty, even though he may be sitting still and doing nothing. But it denotes an energetic power, a continuous activity that works and operates without ceasing. For God does not rest, but works without ceasing, as Christ says in John 5:17: "My Father is working still, and I am working." In the same sense, St. Paul says in Ephesians 3:20: "Now to God who is able to accomplish far more than we can ask"; that is, God always does more than we ask; that is God's way and how God's power works. That is why I said Mary does not desire to be an idol; she does nothing, God does all. We ought to call upon her that for her sake God may grant and do what we request. In this way, all other saints are to be invoked, so that the work may be every way God's alone.

Therefore she adds, "And God's name is holy." That is to say: "As I lay no claim to the work, neither do I to the name and fame. For name and fame belong to God alone, who does the work. It is not proper that one should do the work and another have the fame and take the glory. I am but the workshop in which God performs God's works. I had nothing to do with the work itself. No one should praise me or give me the glory for becoming the Mother of God, but God alone and God's work are to be honored and praised in me. It is enough to congratulate me and call me blessed because God used me and worked in me." Behold how completely she traces all to God, lays claim to no works, no honor, no fame. She conducts herself as before, when she still had nothing of all this: she demands no higher honors than before. She is not puffed up, does not vaunt herself or proclaim with a loud voice that she is become the Mother of God. She seeks not any glory, but goes about her usual household duties, milking the cows, cooking the meals, washing pots and kettles, sweeping out the rooms, and performing the work of maid-servant or housemother in lowly and despised tasks, as though she cared nothing for such great gifts and graces. She was esteemed among other women and her neighbors no more highly than before, nor desired to be, but remained a poor townswoman, one of the great multitude. Oh, how simple and pure a heart was hers, how strange a soul was this! What great things are hidden here under this lowly exterior! How many came in contact with her, talked, and ate and drank with her who perhaps despised her and counted her but a common, poor, and simple village maiden and who, had they known, would have fled from her in terror.

That is the meaning of the clause; "God's name is holy." For "holy" means "separated," "dedicated to God," that none should touch or defile it but all should hold it in honor. And "name" means a good report, fame, praise, and honor. In this way, everyone should let God's name alone, not lay hands on it to appropriate it to oneself. It is a symbol of this when we read in Exodus 30:25–32 that Moses made an oil of holy oint-ment, at God's command, and strictly forbade that it be poured on anyone's flesh. That is, no one should ascribe to oneself the name of God. For we desecrate God's name when we let ourselves be praised or honored, or when we take plea-sure in ourselves and boast of our works or our possessions, as is the way of the world, which constantly dishonors and desecrates the name of God. And all who hallow God's name and deny themselves all honor and glory, rightly honor God's name, and therefore are made holy by it. In this way, we read in Exodus 30:29 that the precious ointment was so holy that it made whatever it touched holy. That is, when God's name is made holy by us, so that we lay claim to no work, fame, or self-satisfaction in it, it is rightly honored, and in turn touches and makes us holy.

Therefore, we must be on our guard because we cannot do without God's good things while we live on earth, and therefore, we cannot be without name and honor. When oth-ers accord us praise and honor, we ought to profit by the example of the Mother of God and at all times arm ourselves with this verse to make the proper reply and to use such honor and praise correctly….

God's mercy is for those who fear God from generation to generation.

We must accustom ourselves to the scriptural usage according to which generations are, as we have said above, the succession of those born in the course of nature, one human being descending from another. Hence, the German word *Geschlechter* is not an adequate translation, though I do not know a better one. For by *Geschlechter* we understand fam-ilies or blood relations. But the word here means the natural succession from father to son and son's son, each several members being called a generation, so that the following would not be a bad translation: "and God's mercy endures to children's children of those who fear God." This is a very common expression in Scripture, with its origin in the Words of God under the First Commandment, spoken on Mount Sinai to Moses and all the people (Exod 20:5–6): "You shall not bow down to them or worship them; for I the Lord your God am a jealous God, punishing children for the iniquity of parents, to the third and fourth generation of those who reject me, but showing steadfast love to the thousandth generation of those who love me and keep my commandments."

Having finished singing about herself and the good things she had from God, and having sung God's praises, Mary now rehearses all the works of God that God works in general in all people, and sings God's praises also for them, teaching us to understand the work, method, nature, and will of God. Many philosophers and persons of great acumen have also engaged in the endeavor to find out the nature of God; they have written much about God—one in this way, another in that—yet all have gone blind over their task and failed of the proper insight. And, indeed, it is the greatest thing in heaven and on earth, to know God correctly, if that may be granted to one. This the Mother of God teaches us here in a masterly fashion, if we would only listen, just as she taught the same above, in and by her own experience. How can one know God better than in the works in which God is most God's very self? Whoever understands God's works correctly cannot fail to know God's nature and will, heart, and mind. To understand God's work is an art. And in order that we learn it, Mary enumerates, in the following four verses, six divine works among as many classes of persons. She divides all the world into two parts and assigns to each side three works and three classes of persons, so that either side has its exact counterpart in the other. She describes the works of God in each of these two parts, portraying God so well that it could not be done better.

This division is well conceived and is borne out by other passages of Scripture. For instance, God says in Jeremiah 9:23–24: "Do not let the wise boast in their wisdom, do not let the mighty boast in their might, do not let the wealthy boast in their wealth; but let those who boast boast in this, that they understand and know me, that I am the Lord. I act with steadfast love, justice, and righteousness in the earth, for in these things I delight, says the Lord." This is a noble text and agrees with this hymn of the Mother of God. Here we see that God too divides all that is in the world into three parts—wisdom, might, and riches—and puts them all down by saying no one should glory in these things, for no one will find God in them, nor does God delight in them. Over against these, God sets three others—kindness, justice, and righteousness. "In these things," God says, "I am to be found; indeed, I practice them, so near am I to them; nor do I practice them in heaven, but in the earth, where people may find me. And in this way whoever understands me may glory and trust in that fact." For if they are not wise but poor in spirit, my kindness is with them, and if they are not mighty but brought low, my justice is by their side to save them; if they are not rich but poor and needy, the more they have of my righteousness.

Under wisdom, God includes all spiritual possessions and gifts, by which a person may gain popularity, fame, and a good report, as the following verse will show. Such gifts are intellect, reason, wit, knowledge, piety, virtue, a godly life, in short, whatever is in the soul that people call divine and spiritual, all great and high gifts, yet none of them God. Under might, God includes all authority, nobility, friends, high station, and honor, whether pertaining to temporal or to spiritual goods or persons, though there is in Scripture no spiritual authority or power, but only servants and subjects—together with all the rights, liberties, and privileges pertaining to them. Under riches are included good health, beauty, pleasure, strength, and every external good that may befall the body. Opposed to these three are the poor in spirit, the oppressed, and those who lack the necessities of life.[32]

SERMON AT COBURG

EDITORS' INTRODUCTION: *This sermon, based upon a harmony of Matthew 27, Luke 25, and John 19, was preached on the day after Luther arrived at the Coburg Castle, where he stayed during the Diet of Augsburg. The congregation included such personages as the Elector John, Count Albrecht of Mansfeld, Philipp Melanchthon, Justus Jonas, Veit Dietrich, and John Agricola. Notes on the sermon were recorded by Veit Dietrich, who prepared the printed version of 1530.*[1]

According to the sermon, Christians must suffer; however, the cross they carry cannot be self-selected but is given to them by the devil and the world. They recognize the unsurpassed gift that Christ has become theirs in his suffering and serving. Thus Christ's suffering is so powerful that "it fills heaven and earth and tears apart the power and might of the devil, hell, death, and sin." When one's suffering and affliction is at its worst, if one can think on Christ, God, who is faithful, comes to help, as God has helped God's own from the beginning of the world. To explain this, Luther invokes the legend of St. Christopher, a story by which simple people can have an example of the Christian life and how it should be lived. When one puts Christ, the dear child, on one's back, one must either carry him all the way through the water or drown. Christopher sinks, but he has a tree on which to cling, which is the promise that Christ will do something special with our suffering. In the world are trials and tribulations, but in Christ one has freedom: "In our drowning we have the tree to which we can cling against the waves, namely, the word and the fine, strong promises that we shall not be over-whelmed by the waves."[2]

APRIL 16, 1530

A SERMON IN PASSION WEEK ON SUFFERING AND THE CROSS

Dear friends, you are aware that the passion is a time for preaching. Thus, I do not doubt that you have heard the nature of this passion and suffering many times and the purpose for which God the Father ordained it. It is that God wanted not the passion of Christ but to help, because it was not Christ but we and the whole human race who deserved this suffering. Furthermore, it is intended as a gift, given out of grace and mercy. This aspect we will not treat now, since I have spoken much about it already. We have many wayward fanatics about, who dishonor the gospel and do us ill by asserting that we know nothing of teaching and preaching except about faith, as if we leave out the teachings about good works and suffering. They also say that they have the right spirit to proclaim such things. Therefore, we now want to speak about the example of the passion—what kind of cross we carry and suffer, and how we should carry and suffer it.

First, we must note that Christ's suffering did not just deliver us from the devil, death, and sins; his suffering is also an example for us that we should follow in our own suffering. Even though our suffering should not be overblown, such that through it we should be saved or earn the tiniest merit, we should nevertheless imitate Christ so that we may be conformed to him. For God decided not only that we should believe in the crucified Christ, but that we should also be crucified with him and suffer with him, as he clearly shows in many places in the Gospels. "Whoever does not take up the cross and follow me," says the Lord, "is not worthy of me" [Matt 10:38]. And again, "If they have called the master of the house Beelzebul, how much more will they malign those of his household!" (Matt 10:25). Therefore, each one must carry a piece of the holy cross, and it cannot be otherwise. St. Paul says as well, "In my flesh I am completing what is lacking in Christ's afflictions" [Col 1:24]. It is as if he were saying that his whole Christianity is not yet completely prepared, and we also must follow so that nothing is lost or lacking from the cross of Christ, but all brought together into one heap. Everyone must ponder that the cross cannot remain external.

Moreover, it has to be such a cross and suffering that it has a name and honestly grips and hurts, such as some great danger to property and honor, or body and life. This is the kind of suffering that one really feels, and it hurts, because it would not be suffering if it did not hurt very much.

However, it should be the kind of suffering that we ourselves do not choose, as the fanatics choose their own suffering. It should be the kind of suffering that, if it were possible, we would gladly be rid of, that the devil or the world gives us. Then it is important, as I said before, that we hold fast and stick to the knowledge that we must suffer to be conformed to Christ,[3] so that it cannot be otherwise that each one must experience a cross and suffering. When one knows this, it is easier and more bearable, and one can comfort oneself by saying, "Well, if I want to be a Christian, I must wear the colors of the court. The dear Christ issues no others in his court; there must be suffering."

The fanatics who pick their own crosses cannot do this; rather, they become stubborn about it and resist. What a pretty and praiseworthy suffering this is, and still they blame us, as if we do not teach correctly about suffering, for they alone know it. We teach, however, that no one should pick up or choose a cross or suffering, but when it comes, it should be carried and endured with patience.

Nevertheless, they do not err only in that they have a self-selected cross, but also in that they exalt their suffering so highly and award themselves great merit, thereby blaspheming God because it is not a true but a stinking, self-selected suffering. We, however, say that we earn nothing from our suffering, and we do not display it in beautiful monstrances as they do. It is enough for us to know that it pleases God that we suffer, so that we are conformed to Christ, as I have said. Thus we see that those who boast and teach the most about suffering and the cross know the least about either the cross or Christ, because they make their own suffering meritorious. This is not what it is about, nor is one pressured or forced to suffer. If you do not want to do it for nothing and without any merit, then you can let it lie and so deny Christ. The way is at the door. If you do not wish to suffer, you simply need to know that you are not worthy of the court. So you can choose between the two, either to suffer or to deny Christ.

If you wish to suffer, so be it. The treasure and comfort that is promised and given you is so great that you ought indeed to suffer gladly and with joy, because Christ together with all his suffering is given to you and becomes your own. If you can believe this, you can freely say in the greatest fear and crisis, "Even if I suffer for a long time, how can it compare to the treasure that my God has given as my possession, namely, that I will live with my God eternally?" Thus, suffering becomes sweet and light, not eternal suffering but a snippet that lasts a moment and passes away. It is as St. Paul [2 Cor 4:17] and St. Peter [1 Pet 1:6] and Christ himself says in the Gospels [John 16:16–22]; they recognize the unsurpassed gift that Christ has become ours in his suffering and serving. Thus, Christ's suffering is so powerful that it fills heaven and earth and tears apart the power and might of the devil, hell, death, and sin. When you hold up your treasure in the face of your affliction and suffering, it seems to be such a small loss over against such a great good to lose a little property, honor, health, spouse, child, your own body and life. If you refuse to regard this treasure and to suffer for it, so be it, go on and let it lie; the one who does not believe will not partake of these unspeakable goods and gifts.

Furthermore, every Christian should attend to the fact and certainly understand that this suffering will turn out for the best, because on account of his word, Christ will not only help to bear such suffering but also turn and transform it for the best. By this means, again, such a cross should become so much sweeter and more bearable, because our loving God wants to pour so many spices and salt-water into our hearts so that we can carry all our afflictions and burdens. As St. Paul says (1 Cor 10:13), "God is faithful, and will not let you be tested beyond your strength, but with the testing will also provide the way out so that you may be able to endure it." This is true when suffering and affliction is at its worst and it stresses and strains one to such a point that one thinks one can stand no more but must drown. If, however, at this point you can think on Christ, God who is faithful comes to help, just as God has helped God's own from the very beginning of the world. For God has remained the same through all the ages, and the cause of our suffering and that of all the saints from the beginning has been the same.

Of course, the whole world must bear witness that we are not suffering because of public scandal or vice, such as adultery, fornication, murder, etc. We suffer because we remain true to God's Word and preach, hear, learn, and practice it. Now, since this is the cause of our suffering, so let it always be; we have the same promise and the same cause for suffering that all the saints then and now have had. Thus, we might also comfort ourselves with the same promise and cling to the same in our suffering and trouble, as is most necessary.

Therefore, we should always pay attention to the promises in relation to our suffering, namely, that our cross and affliction will turn out for the best in a way that we could not wish or imagine. This is exactly what is different between Christian suffering and all other human suffering and afflictions. Other people also have their crosses and tragedies, just as they also can sit in their rose gardens and employ their good fortune and their goods as they please. Nevertheless, when they experience suffering and affliction, they cannot comfort themselves, because they do not have the mighty promises and the trust in God that Christians have; therefore, they cannot console themselves that God will help them carry their afflictions. They can see far less that their afflictions and suffering will turn out for the very best.

Thus, we can see that they cannot overcome even the small afflictions, and when they experience great and powerful afflictions, they despair altogether, commit suicide, or want to die because the world becomes claustrophobic for them. Likewise, they cannot keep a balance, whether in fortune or misfortune....

So that you will understand this better, I will give you an example by which to see how Christian suffering is painted and depicted. You know well how St. Christopher is regularly painted. You should not think that he existed as a man called by that name or who physically did what has been said of him. Nevertheless, the one who created the legend or fable was without doubt a good and reasonable person, who wanted to paint this picture for the simple people so that they would have an example and picture of the Christian life and how it should be lived. He met the mark in painting it. A Christian is like a great giant with great, strong arms and legs, as St. Christopher is painted, because the Christian also bears a burden that the whole world, emperor, king, or prince could not carry. Therefore, each Christian is called Christopher or Christ bearer[4] in that he or she takes up the faith.

How does it work then? When a person takes up the faith, he or she does not think it to be a heavy burden but a small child that is cute and well-formed and easy to carry, as happened for Christopher. At first, the gospel appears to be a dear, friendly, and childlike teaching, as we said at the beginning, as it happened that everyone wanted to be an Evangelical.[5] There was such a hunger and thirst that there could be no oven as heated as the people were then. But how did it go? It turned out just as it did with Christopher; he did not discover how heavy the child was until he was in the deepest part of the water.

So it also went with the gospel as it broke in—the waves came, the pope, bishop, princes, and the rabble set themselves in opposition. Then the child began to feel heavy to carry. [The water] rose so high for the good Christopher that he came close to drowning. As you see, it is happening in the same way now on the other side that is against the Word; there are so many tricks and stratagems, so much deceit and cunning, all aimed to drown us in the water. There is such threat and terror that we might be frightened to death, were it not for the comfort that we have against it.

Consequently, when one puts Christ, the dear child, on one's back, one either has to carry him all the way through the water or drown. There is nothing in between. It is not good to drown; therefore, we want to get through the water with Christ, even if it might seem that we will get stuck in there. We have the promise that one who has Christ can say with David, in the words of Psalm 27[:3], "Though an army encamp against me, my heart shall not fear; though war rise up against me, yet I will be confident." Let them paw and stamp their feet, threaten and frighten as they wish; no matter how deep the water may be, we will go through it with Christ.

So it is with everything else; when it gets going, it becomes too heavy, whether it is sin, the devil, death or hell, or even our own conscience. Well, then, how should one do it? Where should one run for protection? We cannot see it any other way than that the whole thing will collapse. But on their side, they are confident and proud, thinking that they have already won. I also see that the dear Christopher sinks; nevertheless, he comes through it, because he has a tree on which to cling. This tree is the promise that Christ will do something special with our suffering. "In the world," he says, "you will have trials and tribulations, but in me you will have freedom." Similarly, St. Paul writes, "God is faithful and helps us out of affliction, so that we may be able to endure it" [cf. 1 Cor 10:13]. These sayings are branches, even trees, to which one can cling and let the water rush and roar as it will.

Thus, you have an example in Christopher and a picture that can strengthen us in our suffering and teach us that the fear and trembling is not as great as the comfort and the promise. We should know that in this life we will have no rest when we carry Christ, but that in our afflictions we should turn our eyes from the present sufferings and toward the comfort and promise. Then we will learn what Christ says is true; "In me you may have peace" [John 16:33].

This is the manner of the Christian that we all must learn, namely, that we set our eyes on the Word and turn them away from all the attendant and weighty misery and suffering. The flesh cannot attain this manner; it can focus only on the present sufferings. This is the manner of the devil, who shoves the Word far from sight so that one can see nothing but the current misery, just as is true now. What the devil wants is that we should deny and forget the Word altogether and gaze only at the danger around our necks. If he succeeds in this game, he drowns us in misery, so that we see nothing but the rush and roar. But this should not be, for it follows that, if one wants to be a Christian and acts according to feelings, one soon loses Christ. Beat the suffering and the cross from your heart and mind as quickly as you can; otherwise, if you brood over it for a long time, the evil grows worse. If you find yourself in trouble and suffering, then say, "I did not choose and set up this cross for myself; it is the fault of the dear Word of God and because I have and teach Christ that I suffer in this way. So let it go in God's name. I will let God take care of it and fight it out, who said long ago that I would suffer these things and promised me God's gracious help."

If, however, you plunge yourself into the Scriptures, you will feel comfort, and your situation will improve, through which you would otherwise not be able to steer by any act or means on your own. A merchant will, for the sake of money and property, bring himself to leave house and home, wife and child, and risk his life for evil profit without a specific promise or pledge that he will return home healthy to his wife and child; still, he is foolhardy and bold enough to venture into such danger without any promise whatsoever. Now, if a merchant can do that for money and riches, shame on you that we should spurn bearing a little cross and still want to be Christians. Moreover, in our drowning, we have the tree to which we can cling against the waves, namely, the Word, and the fine, strong promises that we shall not be overwhelmed by the waves.

The knight does the same thing. He plunges himself into battle, where innumerable spears, halberds, and firearms are aimed at him. He has no promise by which to console himself except his irrational spirit; nevertheless, he goes forward, even though his whole life is hard and filled with suffering....

Although God does not want to attack and plague us, the devil wants to do exactly that and cannot endure the Word. The devil is by nature so wicked and poisonous, unable to bear anything good, and aggrieved that an apple grows on a tree. It hurts and vexes the devil that you have a healthy finger, and if he could, he would throw everything down and tear it apart. Nothing, however, is more hateful to the devil than the dear Word, and that is because, while the devil can hide under all creatures, the Word uncovers him, such that he cannot hide and everyone knows how evil he is. Then the devil fights back and resists and draws the bishops and princes together and thinks that he has again concealed himself. Nevertheless, it does not help; the Word drags him out into the light. Therefore, the devil does not rest, and because the gospel will not suffer him, he will not suffer the gospel. If our dear God did not protect us through the angels and we were able to see the devil's cunning blows and deceit, we should die from the sight alone, as many are the cannons and guns he has ranged against us. But God protects us so that they do not hit us.

Thus, the two champions clash, and as each does as much as possible, the devil brews one calamity after another, because he is a mighty, wicked, and restless spirit. Now it is time for our dear God to be concerned about God's honor. The word with which we fight is a weak and miserable word, and we who have it and proclaim it are also weak and miserable people and carry this treasure in clay jars [2 Cor 4:7], as Paul says, that can be easily shattered and broken. Therefore, the evil spirit spares no effort and confidently lashes out to break the little vessel; for there it is under his nose, and he cannot stand it. Thus, the struggle begins with water and fire to dampen and drown the little spark.

For a while our dear God looks on and lets us lie between a rock and a hard place, and from our experience, we learn that the weak, suffering word is stronger than the devil and hell's gates. The devil and his followers can storm the fortress all they want. They will find something there that will make them break into a sweat and still not win the day; it is a rock, as Christ calls it, that cannot be overcome. Thus, let us suffer what we will; we will experience that God will stand by us to guard and protect us against the enemy and all his followers.

Third, it is important to note that we do not suffer only to demonstrate God's honor, might, and strength over against the devil, but also because this treasure that we have, when it is not accompanied by danger and suffering, causes us to become sleepy and secure. We see all too commonly that they so misuse the holy gospel that it becomes sin and shame, as if they are so liberated by the gospel that they do not need to do anything, give anything, or suffer anything.

God can only stem this wickedness through the cross. Therefore, God must discipline and drive us, so that our faith grows and becomes stronger and we bring the Savior deeper into our hearts. Just as we cannot live without eating and drinking, so we also cannot live without affliction and suffering. Therefore, we must experience peril from the devil through persecution or a secret thorn piercing our hearts, as St. Paul laments (cf. 2 Cor 12:7). Since it is better to have a cross than not to have one, no one should be upset or terrified over it. You have a good, strong promise on which and by which you can comfort yourself. Besides, the gospel cannot come out in the open except through suffering and the cross.

Lastly, Christian suffering is more noble and more exquisite than any other human suffering because, since

Christ himself suffered, he made all Christian suffering holy. Are we not poor and mad people? We run to Rome, Trier, and other such places to visit the shrines; why do we not also cherish the cross and suffering to which Christ was much closer? These touched him more than some piece of clothing touched his body, touching not only his body but also his heart. Through the suffering of Christ, the suffering of all his saints has become completely holy, for it has been touched by Christ's suffering. Therefore, we should accept all suffering as a holy thing, for it is true holiness.

Since we know that it is God's good pleasure that we suffer, and God's honor is revealed and seen in our suffering better than in any other way, and since we are the kind of people who would not remain in the Word without some suffering, and since we have, nevertheless, the precious and true promise that the cross that God sends us is not an evil thing but a completely exquisite and noble holy thing, why then should we avoid suffering? Let the one who does not want to suffer go and be a knight; we will preach only to those who want to be Christians. The others would not carry this out anyway. We have ample comfort and promise that God will not leave us stuck in suffering but will help us out, even if all manner of people would doubt this.

Thus, even though it hurts, you must suffer somewhat; things cannot always be on an even plain. It is as good—in fact, a thousand times better—to suffer for Christ, who gives us comfort and help in our suffering, than to suffer for the devil and despair and perish.

See, in this way, we learn from the cross, and you need to learn to distinguish carefully the passion of Christ from all other suffering. The former is heavenly; the latter is worldly. His suffering accomplishes everything; ours nothing, except as we are formed in the image of Christ. The suffering of Christ is noble suffering; ours is that of a slave.

Those who teach something else know nothing of Christ's suffering, nor ours. Reason knows nothing else; it wants to obtain merits through its suffering and all its other works. Therefore, we must make distinctions. Now we have spoken enough about the example of the passion and our suffering. May God grant that we learn and comprehend it properly.

THE SACRAMENT OF PENANCE

By Doctor Martin Luther L. A. W.[1]

1. Forgiveness in the Sacrament of Penance is of two kinds: forgiveness of the punishment and forgiveness of the guilt. Concerning the first, the forgiveness of the punishment, or satisfaction, enough has been said in the treatise on indulgences, which appeared some time ago. It is not very significant and is an immeasurably lesser thing than the forgiveness of guilt, which one might call a godly or heavenly indulgence, one that only God can grant from heaven.

2. The difference between these two types of forgiveness is this: the indulgence, or the forgiveness of punishment, does away with works and efforts of satisfaction[2] that have been imposed and thus reconciles a person outwardly with the Christian Church. But the forgiveness of guilt, the heavenly indulgence, does away with the heart's fear and timidity before God; it makes the conscience glad and joyful within and reconciles us with God. And this is what true forgiveness of sins really means, that a person's sins no longer bite or make uneasy, but rather that the joyful confidence overwhelms us because God has forgiven us our sins forever.

3. However, as persons we do not find within ourselves such a [glad] conscience nor do we rejoice in ourselves over God's grace, and that cannot be helped by any indulgence

even though we were to buy all the letters of indulgence ever issued. For we can be saved quite apart from any letters of indulgence, by death making satisfaction or paying for our sin. No one can be saved, however, without a joyful conscience and a glad heart toward God (that is, without the forgiveness of guilt). So it would be much better to buy no indulgences at all, then to forget this forgiveness of guilt or omit to practice it first and foremost every day.

4. For [attaining] such forgiveness of guilt and for calming the heart in the face of its sins, there are various ways and methods. Some think to accomplish this through letters of indulgence. They run to and fro, to Rome or to St. James,[3] buying indulgences here and there. But this is mistaken and all in vain. Things thereby get much worse, for God's very self must forgive sins and grant peace to the heart. Some put themselves out with many good works, even too much fasting and straining. Some have ruined their bodies and gone out of their minds, thinking by virtue of their works to do away with their sins and soothe their heart. Both of these types are defective in that they want to do good works before their sins are forgiven, whereas on the contrary, sins must be forgiven before good works can be done. For works do not drive out sin, but the driving out of sin leads to good works. For good works must be done with a joyful heart and good conscience toward God, that is, out of the forgiveness of guilt.

5. The true way and the right method, without which there is no other, is that most worthy gracious, and holy Sacrament of Penance,[4] which God gave for the comfort of all sinners when he gave the keys to St. Peter in behalf of the whole Christian Church and in Matthew 16[:19], said, "Whatever you bind on earth shall be bound in heaven, and whatever you loose on earth shall be loosed in heaven." This holy, comforting, and gracious Word of God must enter deeply into the heart of every Christian, where we may with great

gratitude let it become part of us. For the Sacrament of Penance consists in this: forgiveness of sin, comfort and peace of conscience, besides joy and blessedness of heart over against all sins and terrors of conscience, as well as against all despair and assaults anxiety and terror [*anfechtung*] brought by the gates of hell [Matt 18:18].[5]

6. Now there are three things in the holy Sacrament of Penance. The first is absolution. These are the words of the priest which show, tell, and proclaim to you that you are free and that your sins are forgiven you by God according to and by virtue of the above-quoted words of Christ to St. Peter. The second is grace, the forgiveness of sins, the peace and comfort of the conscience, as the words declare. This is why it is called a sacrament, a holy sign, because in it one hears the words externally that signify spiritual gifts within, gifts by which the heart is comforted and set at peace. The third is faith, which firmly believes that the absolution and the words of the priest are true, by the power of Christ's words, "Whatever you loose...shall be loosed," etc.

Everything then depends on this faith, which alone makes the sacraments accomplish that which they signify, and everything that the priest says comes true. For as you believe, so it is done for you.[6] Without this faith, all absolution and all sacraments are in vain and indeed do more harm than good. There is a common saying among the teachers that goes like this: not the sacrament, but the faith that believes the sacrament is what removes sin. St. Augustine says this: The sacrament removes sin, not because it takes place, but because it is believed.[7] For this reason, in the sacrament one must studiously discern faith, and this we would now sketch out further.

7. It follows, then, in the first place, that the forgiveness of guilt, the heavenly indulgence, is granted to no one on account of the worthiness of one's contrition over one's sins,

nor on account of one's works of satisfaction, but only on account of one's faith in the promise of God, "Whatever you loose…shall be loosed," etc. Although contrition and good works are not to be neglected, one is nevertheless in no case to build upon them, but only upon the sure words of Christ, who pledges to you that when the priest looses [unbinds] you, you shall be loosed. Your contrition and works may deceive you, and the devil will very soon overturn them in [the hour of death] and of assaults of doubt and temptation [*anfechtung*]. But Christ, your God, will not lie to you, nor will he waver; neither will the devil overturn his words for him. If you build upon them with a firm faith, you will be standing on the rock against which the gates and all the powers of hell cannot prevail [Matt 16:18].

8. It follows further that the forgiveness of guilt is not within the province of any human office or authority, be it pope, bishop, priest, or any other. Rather, it depends exclusively upon the word of Christ, and your own faith. For Christ did not intend to base our comfort, our salvation, our confidence on human words or deeds, but only upon himself, upon his words and deeds. Priests, bishops, and popes are only servants who hold before you the words of Christ, upon which you should depend and rely with firm faith as upon a solid rock. Then the Word will sustain you, and so your sins will have to be forgiven. Moreover, this is why the Word is not to be honored for the sake of priests, bishops, or popes; but priests, bishops, and popes are to be honored for the sake of the Word, as those who bring to you the Word and message of your God that you are loosed from your sins.

9. It follows in addition that in the Sacrament of Penance and forgiveness of guilt, a pope or bishop does nothing more than the lowliest priest. Indeed, where there is no priest, each individual Christian—even a woman or child—does as much. For any Christian can say to you, "God forgives you

your sins, in the name," etc., and if you can accept that word with a confident faith, as though God were saying it to you, then in that same faith, you are surely absolved. So completely does everything depend on faith in God's Word. No pope, bishop, or priest can do anything to your faith. Neither can anyone give to another any better Word of God than that common word he spoke to Peter, "Whatever you loose... shall be loosed." This word must be in every absolution; indeed, every absolution depends upon it.

Even so, one should observe and not despise the established orders of authority. Only, make no mistake about the sacrament and its effect, as if it counted for more when given by a bishop or a pope than when given by a priest or a layperson. As the priest's Mass and baptism and distribution of the holy body of Christ is just as valid as if the pope or bishop were doing it, so it is with absolution, that is, the Sacrament of Penance. The fact that they reserve certain cases for absolution does not make their sacrament any greater or better. It is the same as if for some reason they withheld from anybody the Mass, baptism, or the like. Nothing would thereby be either added to or taken away from baptism and the Mass.

10. Therefore, if you believe the word of the priest when he absolves you (that is, when he looses you in the name of Christ and in the power of his words saying, "I absolve you from your sins"), then your sins are assuredly absolved also before God, before all angels and all creatures—not for your sake, or for the priest's sake, but for the sake of the very word of Christ, who cannot be lying to you when he says, "Whatever you loose...shall be loosed." Should you, however, not believe that your sins are truly forgiven and removed, then you are a heathen, acting toward your Lord Christ like one who is an unbeliever and not a Christian; and this the most serious sin of all against God. Besides, you had better not go to the priest if you will not believe his absolution; you will be

doing yourself great harm by your disbelief. By such disbelief, you make your God to be a liar when, through God's priest, God says to you, "You are loosed from your sins," and you retort, "I don't believe it," or, "I doubt it." As if you were more certain in your opinion than God is in God's words, whereas you should be letting personal opinions go, and with unshakeable faith giving place to the Word of God spoken through the priest. For if you doubt whether your absolution is approved of God and whether you are rid of your sins, that is the same as saying, "Christ has not spoken the truth, and I do not know whether he approves his own words, when he says to Peter, 'Whatever you loose...shall be loosed.'" O God, spare everybody from such diabolical disbelief.

11. When you are absolved from your sins, indeed when amid your awareness of sin, some devout Christian—man or woman, young or old—comforts you, then receive this absolution in such faith that you would readily let yourself be torn apart or killed over and over again, or readily renounce everything else, rather than doubt that you have been truly absolved before God. Since by God's grace it is commanded of us to believe and to hope that our sins are forgiven us, how much more then ought you to believe it when God gives you a sign of it through another person! There is no greater sin than not to believe this article of "the forgiveness of sins," which we pray daily in the Creed. And this sin is called the sin against the Holy Spirit. It strengthens all other sins and makes them forever unforgivable. Consider, therefore, what a gracious God and Father we have. God not only promises us forgiveness of sins, but also commands us, on pain of committing the most grievous sin of all, to believe that they are forgiven. With this same command, God constrains us to have a joyful conscience while using this terrible sin as a means of driving us away from sins and from a bad conscience.[8]

12. Some people have been teaching us that we should, and must necessarily, be uncertain about absolution, and doubt whether we have been restored to grace and our sins forgiven—on the grounds that we do not know whether our contrition has been adequate or whether sufficient satisfaction has been made for our sins.[9] Because this is not known, the priest cannot at once assign appropriate penance. Be on guard against these misleading and un-Christian gossips. The priest is necessarily uncertain as to your contrition and faith, but this is not what matters. To him, it is enough that you make confession and seek an absolution. He is supposed to give it to you and is obligated to do so. What will come of it, however, he should leave to God and to your faith. You should not be debating in the first place whether or not your contrition is sufficient. Rather, you should be assured of this, that after all your efforts, your contrition is not sufficient. This is why you must cast yourself upon the grace of God, hear God's sufficiently sure Word in the sacrament, accept it in free and joyful faith, and never doubt that you have come to grace—not by your own merits or contrition but by God's gracious and divine mercy, which promises, offers, and grants you full and free forgiveness of sins in order that in the face of all the assaults, anxiety and doubt [*anfechtungen*] of sin, conscience, and the devil, you thus learn to glory and trust not in yourself or your own actions, but in the grace and mercy of your dear Father in heaven. After that, be contrite all the more and render satisfaction as well as you can. Only, let this simple faith in the unmerited forgiveness promised in the words of Christ go before and remain in command of the situation.

13. Those, however, who do not desire peace think then that they have produced adequate contrition and works—beyond that, they make Christ a liar and flirt with the sin against the Holy Spirit, in addition to treating the

most worthy Sacrament of Penance unworthily. So they receive their deserved reward: they build on sand [Matt 7:26], trusting themselves more than God. The result must necessarily be an ever greater uneasiness of conscience, a vain striving after impossible things, a quest for assurance and comfort that they never find. Such a perversion issues finally in despair and eternal damnation. For what else are they seeking but a certainty achieved by their own efforts? As though they wanted by their own works to reinforce God's Word, through which they are supposed to be strengthened in faith—and begin to buttress heaven, to which they should be clinging for their own support. That is, they will not let God be merciful. They want God only for judge, as if God should not forgive anything freely unless it were first recompensed. Yet, in the entire gospel, we read of no one of whom God required anything but faith; out of grace God bestowed all God's benefits full and free upon the unworthy, bidding them afterward to live uprightly and to go in peace, etc.

14. Do not worry about whether a priest in his absolution errs, is himself bound [Matt 16:19], or is merely jesting. If you just receive the words sincerely and believe them, as long as you neither know nor despise his error or bond, you are nevertheless absolved and have the full sacrament. For, as already indicated, this sacrament does not depend on the priest nor on your own actions, but entirely on your faith, you have as much as you believe. Without this faith, you could have all the contrition in the world, but it would still be only the remorse of Judas that angers rather than reconciles God. For nothing reconciles God better than when one gives God the honor that God is truthful and gracious; and no one does this except the one who believes God's Words. Thus, David praises God, "Lord you are slow to anger, merciful, and truthful."[10] This same truth saves us from all sins. If we cling to it by faith.

15. It follows that the keys or authority of St. Peter is not an authority at all but a service, and the keys have not been given to St. Peter but to you and me. The keys are yours and mine. For St. Peter, insofar as he is a pope or a bishop, does not need them; to him they are neither necessary nor helpful. Their entire value lies rather in this, that they help sinners by comforting and strengthening their conscience. Thus Christ ordered that authority in the church should be a rendering of service; and by means of the keys, the clergy should be serving not themselves but only us. For this reason, as one sees, the priest does no more than to speak a word, and the sacrament is already there. This word is God's Word, even as God has promised. The priest, moreover, has sufficient evidence and reason to grant absolution when he sees that one desires it from him. Beyond that, he is not obligated to know anything. I say this in order that the most gracious virtue of the keys should be cherished and honored, and not despised because of abuse by some who do little more than threaten, annoy, and pronounce the ban. They create nothing but tyranny out of this lovely and comforting authority, as if Christ were thinking only of the will and domination of the priests when he instituted the keys and did not even know to what use they should put it.

16. Just so no one accuses me again of forbidding good works, let me say that one should with all seriousness be contrite and remorseful, confess and do good works. This I maintain, however, as best I can: that in the sacrament, we let faith be the chief thing, the legacy through which one may attain the grace of God. After that, we can do a lot of good works—to the glory of God alone and to the benefit of our neighbors, and not in order that we might depend upon that as sufficient to pay for our sin. For God gives us grace freely and without cost; so we should also serve God freely and without cost.

Besides, everything that I have said about this sacrament is said to them whose conscience is troubled, uneasy, erring, and terrified, who would gladly be loosed from their sin and be righteous, but who do not know where to begin. For those are the ones who likewise have true contrition, indeed they are too contrite and fainthearted. God comforts people like those through the Prophet Isaiah, chapter 40, "Cry to the fainthearted and say to them, *consolamini*, be comforted, you faint of heart, behold your God."[11] In Matthew 11[:28], Christ says, "Come to me, you who are burdened and troubled, I will comfort you," etc. The hardhearted, however, who do not as yet seek comfort for their conscience, have likewise not yet experienced this tormenting anxiety. To them this sacrament is of no use. One must first soften them up with the terrible judgment of God and cause them to quail, so that they too may learn to sigh, and seek for the comfort of this sacrament.

17. In confession, if a priest wishes to inquire, or if you want to examine yourself, as to whether or not you are truly contrite, I have no objections. Just so no one becomes so bold in the sight of God that one claims to have sufficient contrition. Such an attitude is presumptuous and fabricated, for no one has sufficient contrition for one's sin. The inquiry could even be greatly exaggerated as whether a person firmly believes the sacrament, that one's sins are forgiven as Christ said to the paralytic, "My son, have faith and your sins are forgiven you." [Matt 9:2]; and to the woman, "Have faith my daughter, your faith has made you well" [Matt 9:22]. Such inquiry has become quite rare in this sacrament; we operate only with contrition, sin, satisfaction, and indulgence. So the blind keep leading the blind [Matt 15:14]. Actually, in this sacrament, the priest, in his word, brings God's message about sin and the forgiveness of guilt. Hence, he should indeed be the one who inquires and discerns most of all

whether a person is receptive to the message. Such receptivity can never consist in anything other than faith and the desire to receive this message. Sin, contrition, and good works should be treated in sermons before the sacrament and confession.

18. It may happen that God does not cause a person to find the forgiveness of guilt, and the turbulence and uneasiness of conscience persist after the sacrament as before. Here one must deal wisely, for the fault is in the faith. It is just as impossible that the heart should not be joyful when it believes its sins are forgiven, as that it should not be troubled and uneasy when it believes its sins are unforgiven. Now, if God allows faith to remain weak, one should not despair on that account, but rather recognize it as a trial and an assault of temptation [*anfechtung*] by means of which God tests, prods, and drives a person to cry out all the more and plead for such faith, saying with the father of the possessed boy in the Gospel, "O Lord, help my unbelief" [Mark 9:24] and with the apostles, "O Lord, increase our faith" [Luke 17:5]. Thus does a person come to learn that everything depends on the grace of God: the sacrament, the forgiveness, and the faith. Giving up all other hope, despairing of oneself, one comes to hope exclusively in the grace of God and clings to it without ceasing.

19. Now penance and the Sacrament of Penance are two different matters. As said above,[12] the sacrament consists in three things, in the Word of God, that is, the absolution; in the faith [which trusts] in this absolution; and in the peace, that is, the forgiveness of sins which surely follows faith. But penance has also been divided into three "parts": contrition, confession, and satisfaction.

Now just as in contrition there is many an abuse, as has already been noted, so it is also in the case of confession and satisfaction. There are a host of books on these subjects,[13] but unfortunately very few on the Sacrament of Penance. Where, however, the sacrament proceeds correctly in faith, there penance—confession, contrition, and satisfaction—is a less weighty matter, and there is no danger of there being too little or too much. For the faith of the sacrament makes all the crooked straight and fills up all the uneven ground. So no one who has this sacramental faith can err, whether in contrition, confession, or satisfaction; and even if one does err, it does one no harm. Where there is no faith, however, there neither contrition, nor confession, nor satisfaction is adequate. For this reason, so many books and teachings appear on contrition, confession, and satisfaction. These serve only to frighten into confessing often, whether the sins they confess are venial or mortal, they do not know. Yet, this time we desire to say a little more about the subject.

20. Venial sins one need not confess to the priest, but only to God. Now, however, another question arises: What are mortal and venial sins? There has never yet been a teacher, nor will there ever be one, learned enough to give us a dependable rule for distinguishing venial from mortal sins, except in such obvious offenses against God's commandments as adultery, murder, theft, falsehood, slander, betrayal, hatred, and the like. It is, moreover, entirely up to God to judge which other sins he regards as mortal. Nor is it possible for us to recognize this, as Psalm 19[:12][14] says, "O God, who can discern all one's sins? Cleanse me from secret sins." Therefore, private confession is no place for [reciting] sins other than those which one openly recognizes as deadly, those which at the time are oppressing and frightening the conscience. For if one were to confess all one's sins, one would have to be confessing every moment, since in this life, we are never without sin. Even our good works are not pure and without sin. Yet it is not fruitless to confess the slighter sins, particularly if one is not aware of any mortal sins. For as

has been said, in this sacrament, God's Word is heard, and [through it] faith is strengthened more and more. Even if one should have nothing to confess, it would still be profitable for the sake of that very faith to hear often the absolution, God's Word. Thus one would grow accustomed to believing in the forgiveness of sins. This is why I said that the faith of the sacrament does everything even though the confession be too much or too little. Everything is profitable to one who believes God's sacrament and Word.

Concerning satisfaction, let this now suffice: the best kind of satisfaction is to sin no more and to do all possible good toward your neighbor, be they enemy or friend. This kind of satisfaction is rarely mentioned; we think to pay for everything simply through assigned prayers.

21. This is the authority of which Christ speaks, in Matthew 9[:6–8], to the unbelieving scribes, "That you may know that the son of man has authority on earth to forgive sins— he said to the paralytic—'Arise, take up your bed and go home.' And he rose and went home. When the crowds saw it, they were afraid, and they glorified God, who had given such authority to human beings." Now this authority to forgive sins is nothing other than what a priest, indeed, if need be, any Christian, may say to another when that one sees someone afflicted or frightened in sins. One can joyously speak this verdict, "Take heart, your sins are forgiven" [Matt 9:2]. Whoever accepts this and believes it as a Word of God, their sins are surely forgiven.

Where, however, there is no such faith, it would do no good even if Christ or God spoke the verdict. For God cannot give a person something that a person does not want to have. And that person does not want to have it, who does not believe that it is being given to him or her. [In that way, the person] does the Word of God a great dishonor, as was said above.[15] You see, then, that the whole church is full of the forgiveness of sins. But few there are who really accept and receive it. For they do not believe it and would rather rely upon their own works.

So it is true that a priest genuinely forgives sin and guilt, although the priest is in no position to give to the sinner that faith which receives and accepts the forgiveness. For this faith God must give. Nevertheless, the forgiveness is genuine, as true as if God had spoken it, whether it is grasped by faith or not. Such authority to forgive sins, and thus to render a verdict in God's place, no one possessed in the Old Testament, neither high priest nor ordinary priests, neither kings nor prophets, nor anyone among the people. The only exceptions occurred at God's express order, as when Nathan confronted King David [2 Sam 12:1–15]. But in the New Testament, every Christian has this authority to forgive sins, where a priest is not at hand. Every Christian has it through the promise of Christ, where he said to Peter, "Whatever you loose on earth shall be loosed in heaven" [Matt 16:19]. Had this been said to Peter alone, then in Matthew 18[:18] Christ would not have said to all in general, "Whatever you loose on earth shall be loosed in heaven." There, Christ is speaking to all Christendom and to each Christian in particular. The great thing about the Christian is that God cannot be fully loved and praised if we are no longer given to hear more than one person speaking to us in such a word. Now the world is full of Christians, yet no one pays any attention to this or gives God thanks.

To sum it all up:

Whoever believes in God— $\begin{cases} \text{everything is helpful,} \\ \text{nothing is harmful.} \end{cases}$

Whoever does not believe in God— $\begin{cases} \text{everything is harmful,} \\ \text{nothing is helpful.} \end{cases}$

THE HOLY AND BLESSED SACRAMENT OF BAPTISM[1]

1519

D(octor) M(artin) A(ugustinian)

1. Baptism [*Die Taufe*] is *baptismos* in Greek and *mersio* in Latin, and means to plunge something completely into the water, so that the water covers it. Although in many places it is no longer customary to thrust and dip infants into the font, but only with the hand to pour the baptismal water upon them out of the font, nevertheless the former is what should be done.[2] It would be proper, according to the meaning of the word *Taufe*, that the infant, or whoever is to be baptized, should be put in and sunk completely into the water and then drawn out again. For even in the German tongue, the word *Taufe* comes undoubtedly from the word *tief* [deep] and means that what is baptized is sunk deeply into the water. This usage is also demanded by the significance of baptism itself. For baptism, as we shall hear, signifies that the old person and the sinful birth of flesh and blood are to be wholly drowned by the grace of God. We should, therefore, do justice to its meaning and make baptism a true and complete sign of the thing it signifies.

2. Baptism is an external sign or token, which so separates us from all people not baptized that we are known as a people of Christ, our Leader, under whose banner of the holy cross we continually fight against sin. In this holy sacrament, we must, therefore, pay attention to three things: the sign, the significance of it, and the faith.

The sign consists in this, that we are thrust into the water in the name of the Father and of the Son and of the Holy Spirit; however, we are not left there but are drawn out again. This accounts for the expression: *aus der Taufe gehoben.*[3] The sign must thus have both its parts, the putting in and the drawing out.

3. The significance of baptism is a blessed dying unto sin and a resurrection in the grace of God, so that the old person, conceived and born in sin, is there drowned, and a new person, born in grace, comes forth and rises. Thus, Jesus, in John 3[:3, 5], says: "Unless you are born again of water and the Spirit, you may not enter into the kingdom of heaven." For just as a child is drawn out of his mother's womb and is born, and through this fleshly birth is a sinful person and a child of wrath [Eph 2:3], so one is drawn out of baptism and is born spiritually. Through this spiritual birth, one is a child of grace and a justified person. Therefore, sins are drowned in baptism, and in place of sin, righteousness comes forth.

4. This significance of baptism—the dying or drowning of sin—is not fulfilled completely in this life. Indeed, this does not happen until one passes through bodily death and completely decays to dust. As we can plainly see, the sacrament or sign of baptism is quickly over. But the spiritual baptism, the drowning of sin which it signifies lasts as long as we live and is completed only in death. Then it is that a person is completely sunk in baptism, and that which baptism signifies comes to pass.

Therefore, this whole life is nothing else than a spiritual baptism which does not cease until death, and the one who is baptized is condemned to die. It is as if the priest, when he baptizes, were to say, "Lo, you are sinful flesh. Therefore, I drown you in God's name and in God's name condemn you to death, so that with you all your sins may die and be destroyed." So St. Paul, in Romans 8[6:4], says: "We were buried with Christ by baptism into death." The sooner a person dies after baptism, the sooner is that person's baptism completed. For sin never ceases entirely while the body lives, which is so wholly conceived in sin that sin is its very nature, as the prophet says [Ps 51:5], "Behold I was conceived in sin, and in iniquity did my mother bear me." There is no help for the sinful nature unless it dies and is destroyed with its sins. Therefore, the life of a Christian, from baptism to the grace, is nothing else than the beginning of a blessed death. For at the last day, God will make one altogether new.

5. Similarly, the lifting up out of the baptismal water is quickly done, but the thing it signifies—the spiritual birth and the increase of grace and righteousness—even though it begins in baptism, lasts until death, indeed, until the last day. Only then will that be finished, which the lifting up out of baptism signifies. Then shall we arise from death, from sins, and from all evil, pure in body and soul, and then shall we live eternally. Then shall we be truly lifted up out of baptism and be completely born, and we shall put on the true baptismal garment of immortal life in heaven. It is as if the sponsors, when they lift the child out of baptism, were to say, "Lo your sins are now drowned, and we receive you in God's name into an eternal life of innocence." For in this way will the angels at the last day raise up all Christians—all the devout baptized—and will there fulfill what baptism and the sponsors signify, as Christ declares in Matthew 24[:31], "God

will send out angels, and they will gather to God the elect from the four winds, from one end of heaven to another."

6. Baptism was foreshadowed of old in Noah's flood, when the whole world was drowned, except for Noah with his three sons and their wives, eight souls, who were saved in the ark. That the people of the world were drowned signifies that in baptism sins are drowned. But that the eight in the ark, with animals of every sort, were preserved, signifies—as St. Peter explains in his second epistle[4]—that through baptism a person is saved. Now, baptism is by far a greater flood than was that of Noah. For that flood drowned people during no more than one year, but baptism drowns all sorts of people throughout the world, from the birth of Christ even until the day of Judgment. Moreover, while that was a flood of wrath, this is a flood of grace, as is declared in Psalm 29[:10],[5] "God will make a continual new flood." For without doubt many more people have been baptized than were drowned in the flood.

7. From this it follows, to be sure, that when someone comes forth out of baptism, one is truly pure, without sin, and wholly guiltless. Still, there are many who do not properly understand this. They think that sin is no longer present, and so they become remiss and negligent in the killing of their sinful nature, even as some do when they have gone to confession. For this reason, as I have said above, it should be properly understood and known that our flesh, so long as it lives here is by nature wicked and sinful.

To correct this wickedness, God has devised the plan of making our flesh altogether new, even as Jeremiah [18:4–6] shows. For the potter when the vessel "was spoiled in his hand" thrust it again into the lump of clay and kneaded it, and afterward made another vessel, as seemed good to him. "So," says God, "are you in my hands." In the first birth, we are spoiled, therefore, God thrusts us into the earth again by death, and makes us over at the last day, that we may be perfect and without sin.

This plan, as has been said, begins in baptism, which signifies death and the resurrection at the last day. Therefore, so far as the sign of the sacrament and its significance are concerned, sins and the person are both already dead, and the person has risen again, and so the sacrament has taken place. But the work of the sacrament has not yet been fully done, which is to say that death and the resurrection at the last day are still before us.

8. A baptized person is, therefore, sacramentally altogether pure and guiltless. This means nothing else than that the person has the sign of God; that is to say, one has the baptism by which it is shown that one's sins are all to be dead, and that one also is to die in grace and at the last day is to rise again to everlasting life, pure, sinless, and guiltless. With respect to the sacrament, then, it is true that one is without sin and guilt. Yet, because all is not yet completed and one still lives in sinful flesh, one is not without sin. But, although not pure in all things, one has begun to grow into purity and innocence.

Therefore, when a person comes to mature age, the natural and sinful appetites—wrath, impurity, lust, greed, pride, and the like—begin to stir; whereas there would be none of these if all sins were drowned in the sacrament and were dead. But the sacrament only signifies that they are to be drowned through the death and the resurrection of the last day. So St. Paul, in Romans 7[:17–20], and the saints with him, lament that they are sinners and have sin in their nature, even though they were baptized and were holy. They lament in this way because the natural and sinful appetites are always active so long as we live.

9. You ask, "How does baptism help me, if it does not altogether blot out and remove sin?" This is the place of a

right understanding of the Sacrament of Baptism. This blessed Sacrament of Baptism helps you because in it God allies God's very self with you and becomes one with you in a gracious covenant of comfort.

In the first place, you give yourself up to the Sacrament of Baptism and what it signifies. That is, you desire to die together with your sins and to be made new at the last day. This is what the sacrament declares, as has been said. God accepts this desire at your hands and grants you baptism. From that hour, God begins to make you a new person. God pours into you God's grace and Holy Spirit, who begins to slay nature and sin and to prepare you for death and the resurrection at the last day.

In the second place, you pledge yourself to continue in this desire, and to slay your sin more and more as long as you live, even until your dying day. This too God accepts. God trains and test you all your life along with many good works and with all kinds of sufferings. In this way, God accomplishes what you in baptism have desired, namely, that you may become free from sin, die, and rise again at the last day, and so fulfill your baptism. Therefore, we read and see how bitterly God has let the saints be tortured and how much God has let them suffer, in order that, almost slain, they might fulfill the Sacrament of Baptism, die, and be made new. For when this does not happen, when we do not suffer and are not tested, then the evil nature gains the upper hand so that a person invalidates his or her baptism, falls into sin, and remains the same old person that they were before.

10. So long as you keep your pledge to God, God in turn gives you grace. God pledges not to impute to you the sins which remain in your nature after baptism, neither to take them into account nor to condemn you because of them. God is satisfied and well pleased if you are constantly striving and desiring to conquer these sins and at your death to

be rid of them. For this reason, although evil thoughts and appetites may be at work, indeed even though at times you may sin and fall, these sins are already broken by the power of the sacrament and covenant. The one condition is that you rise again and enter into the covenant, as St. Paul says in Romans 8[:1]. No one who believes in Christ is condemned by the evil, sinful inclination of one's nature, if only one does not follow it and give in to it. St. John the Evangelist writes in his epistle [1 John 2:1–2], "If any one does sin, we have an advocate with God, even Jesus Christ, who has become the forgiveness of our sins." All this takes place in baptism, where Christ is given us, as we shall hear in the treatise which follows.[6]

11. Now, if this covenant did not exist, and God were not so merciful as to work at our sins, there could be no sin so small but it would condemn us. For the judgment of God can endure no sin. Therefore, there is no greater comfort on earth than baptism. For it is through baptism that we come under the judgment of grace and mercy, which does not condemn our sins but drives them out by many trials. There is a fine sentence of St. Augustine which says, "Sin is altogether forgiven in baptism; not in such a manner that it is no longer present, but in such a manner that it is no longer imputed."[7] It is as if he were to say, "Sin remains in our flesh even until death and works without ceasing. But so long as we do not give our consent to it or desire to remain in it, sin is so overruled by our baptism that it does not condemn us and is not harmful to us. Rather, it is daily being more and more destroyed in us until our death."

For this reason, no one should be terrified if one feels evil lust or love, nor should one despair even if one falls. Rather, one should remember one's baptism, and comfort oneself joyfully with the fact that God has there pledged God's very self to slay one's sin and not to count it a cause for condemnation, if only one does not say yes to sin or remain in it. Moreover, these wild thoughts and appetites, and even a fall into sin, should not be regarded as an occasion for despair. Regard them rather as an admonition from God that we should call upon God's mercy and exercise ourselves in striving against sin, that we should even welcome death in order that we may be rid of sin.

12. Here, then, is the place to discuss the third thing in the sacrament: faith. Faith means that one firmly believes all this: that this sacrament not only signifies death and the resurrection at the last day, but also that it assuredly begins and achieves this; that it establishes a covenant between us and God to the effect that we will fight against sin and slay it, even to our dying breath, while God will be merciful to us, deal graciously with us, and because we are not sinless in this life until purified by death—not judge us with severity.

So you understand how in baptism a person becomes guiltless, pure, and sinless, while at the same time continuing full of evil inclinations. One can be called pure only in the sense that one has started to become pure and has a sign and covenant of this purity and is ever to become more pure. Because of this, God will not count one's former impurity. A person is thus pure by the gracious imputation of God, rather than by virtue of one's own nature. As the prophet says in Psalm 32[:1–2], "Blessed is the one whose transgression is forgiven; blessed is the one to whom the Lord imputes no iniquity."

This faith is of all things the most necessary, for it is the ground of all comfort. One who does not possess such faith must despair of one's sins. For the sin which remains after baptism makes it impossible for any good works to be pure before God. For this reason, we must boldly and without fear hold fast to our baptism, and set it high against all sins and terrors of conscience. We must humbly admit, "I know well that I cannot do a single thing that is pure. But I am baptized, and through my baptism God, who cannot lie, has bound God's very self, in a covenant with me. God will not count my sin against me, but will slay it and blot it out."

13. So, then, we understand that the innocence which is ours by baptism is so called simply and solely because of the mercy of God. For God has begun this work in us, God bears patiently with our sin and regards us as if we were sinless. This also explains why Christians are called in the Scriptures the children of mercy, a people of grace, and people of God's good will.[8] It is because through baptism they have begun to become pure; by God's mercy, with respect to the sins that still remain, they are not condemned; until, finally, through death and at the last day, they become wholly pure just as the sign of baptism shows.

Therefore, those people err greatly who think that through baptism they have become wholly pure. They go about in their ignorance and do not slay their sin. Indeed, they do not admit that it is sin. They simply persist in it, and so make their baptism of no effect. They continue to depend only on a few external works. Meanwhile pride, hatred, and other evils in their nature, which they disregard, grow worse and worse.

How contrary this is! Sin, evil inclination, must be recognized as truly sin. That it does not harm us, however, is to be ascribed to the grace of God. God will not count sin against us if only we keep striving against it with many trials, tasks, and sufferings, and at last slay it at death. To them who do this not, God will not forgive their sins. For they do not live according to their baptism and covenant, and they hinder the work of God and of their baptism, which has been begun.

14. Those who presume to blot out and put away their sin by "satisfaction" are the same sort of people. They go so far as to disregard their baptism, as if they had no more need

of it beyond the fact of having once been baptized. They do not know that baptism is in force all through life, even unto death, yes—as said above—even to the last day. For this reason, they presume to find some other way of blotting out sin, namely, by works. So for themselves and for all others, they create evil, terrified, and uncertain consciences, and despair at the hour of death. They do not know how they stand with God, thinking that by sin they have now lost their baptism and that it profits them no more.

Guard yourself, by all means, against this error. For as has been said, if anyone has fallen into sin, one should all the more remember one's baptism, how God has here made a covenant with that person to forgive all one's sins, if only one would fight against them until death. Upon this truth, upon this alliance with God, one must joyfully dare to rely. The baptism again goes into force and operation. So one's heart again becomes peaceful and glad, not in one's own works or "satisfaction," but in the mercy of God promised to one in baptism, a mercy which God will keep forever. This faith a person must hold so firmly that one would cling to it even though everything and all sins attacked one. For one who is forced away from this faith makes God a liar in God's promise in the Sacrament of Baptism.

15. It is faith like this that the devil attacks most of all. If the devil can overthrow it, the devil has won the battle. For the Sacrament of Penance (of which we have already spoken)[9] also has its foundation in this sacrament, inasmuch as sins are forgiven only to those who are baptized, to those whose sins God has promised to forgive. The Sacrament of Penance thus renews and points out again the Sacrament of Baptism. It is as if the priest, in the absolution, were saying, "Lo, God has now forgiven you your sin, as God long since promised you in baptism, and now God has commanded me, by the power of the keys, to assure you of this forgiveness."

Therefore, you now come again into that which baptism is and does. Believe, and you have it. Doubt, and you are lost. So we find that through sin baptism is indeed hindered in its work, in the forgiveness and the slaying of sin. Yet only by lack of faith in its operation is baptism canceled out. Faith, in turn, removes the hindrance to the operation of baptism. Thus everything depends on faith.

To speak plainly, it is one thing to forgive sins, and another thing to put them away or drive them out. The forgiveness of sins is obtained by faith, even though they are not entirely driven out. But to drive out sins is to exercise ourselves against them, and at last it is to die, for in death, sin perishes completely. But both the forgiveness and the driving out of sins are the work of baptism. Thus the Apostle writes to the Hebrews [12:1], who were baptized and whose sins are forgiven, that they should lay aside the sin which clings to them. For as I believe that God will not count my sins against me, my baptism is in force and my sins are forgiven, even though they may still in a great measure be present. After that follows their driving out through sufferings, death, and the like. This is what we confess in the article [of the Creed], "I believe in the Holy Spirit, the forgiveness of sins," and so forth. Here, there is special reference to baptism, in which the forgiveness takes place through God's covenant with us; therefore, we must not doubt this forgiveness.

16. It follows, then, that baptism makes all sufferings and especially death, profitable and helpful so that they simply have to serve baptism in the doing of its work, that is, in the slaying of sin. It cannot be otherwise. For the one who would fulfill the work and purpose at baptism and be rid of sin, must die. Sin, however, does not like to die, and for this reason, it makes death so bitter and so horrible. Such is the grace and power of God that sin, which has brought death, is driven out again by its very own work, namely, by death itself.

The Holy and Blessed Sacrament of Baptism

You find many people who wish to live in order that they may become righteous and who say that they would like to be righteous. Now there is no shorter way or manner than through baptism and the work of baptism, which is suffering and death. Yet so long as they are not willing to take this away, it is a sign that they do not properly intend or know how to become righteous. Therefore, God has instituted many estates in life in which people are to learn to exercise themselves and to suffer. To some, God has commanded the estate of matrimony, to others the estate of the clergy, to others the estate of temporal rule, and to all God has commanded that they shall toil and labor to kill the flesh and accustom it to death. Because for all who are baptized, their baptism has made the repose, ease, and prosperity of this life a very poison and a hindrance to its work. For, in the easy life, no one learns to suffer, to die with gladness, to get rid of sin, and to live in harmony with baptism. Instead, there grows only love of this life and horror of eternal life, fear of death and unwillingness to blot out sin.

17. Consider now the lives of people. Many there are who fast, pray, go on pilgrimage, and exercise themselves in such things, thinking thereby only to heap up merit and sit down in the high places of heaven; they no longer learn to slay their evil vices. But fasting and all such exercises should be aimed at holding down the old Adam, the sinful nature, and at accustoming it to do without all that is pleasing for this life, and thus preparing it more and more each day for death, so that the work and purpose of baptism may be fulfilled. And all these exercises and toils are to be measured not by their number or by their greatness, but by the demands of baptism. That is to say, everyone is to take upon oneself so much of these works as is good and profitable for the suppressing of one's sinful nature and for the preparation of it for death. One is to increase or to decrease these works

according as one sees sin increasing or diminishing. As it is, people go their way and take upon themselves this, that, and the other task, doing now this, now that, according to the appearance or the reputation of the work. Afterward, they let it drop just as quickly and thus become altogether inconstant, until in the end they amount to nothing. Indeed, some of them so rack their brains over the whole business, and so abuse nature, but they are useless both to themselves and to others.

All this is the fruit of that doctrine with which we have been so infatuated as to think that after repentance or baptism we are without sin and that our good works are to be heaped up for their own sake or as a "satisfaction" for sins already done, but not for the blotting out of sin as such. This is encouraged by those preachers who preach unwisely the legends and the deeds of the blessed saints and hold them up as examples for all. The ignorant easily fall for these things, and effect their own destruction out of the examples of the saints. God has given every saint a special way and a special grace for living according to one's baptism. But baptism and its significance God has set as a common standard for everyone. Each of us is to examine ourselves according to our station in life and is to find out what is the best way to fulfill the work and purpose of our baptisms, namely, to slay sin and to die in order that Christ's burden may thus grow light and easy [Matt 11:30] and not be carried with worry and care. Solomon has this to say of it: "The toil of a fool only wearies one, because one does not know the way to the city" [Eccl 10:15]. For even as they are worried who wish to go to the city and cannot find their way, so it is with these people also; all their life and labor is a burden to them, and yet it accomplishes nothing.

18. In this place, then, belongs the common question whether baptism, and the vow which we make to God, is something more or greater than the vows of chastity, of the

priesthood, or of the clergy. Since baptism is common to all Christians, it is supposed that the clergy have taken a special and a higher vow.

I answer: From what has been said, this is an easy question to answer. For in baptism, we all make one and the same vow: to slay sin and to become holy through the work and grace of God, to whom we yield and offer ourselves, as clay to the potter [Jer 18:4–6]. In this, no one is any better than another. But for a life in accordance with baptism, for the slaying of sin, there can be no one method and no special estate in life. This is why I said that each person must test oneself that one may know in what estate one may best slay sin and put a check upon one's nature. It is true, then, that there is no vow higher, better, or greater than the vow of baptism. What more can we promise than to drive out sin, to die, to hate this life, and to become holy?

Over and above this vow, a person may indeed bind oneself to an estate which will be suitable and helpful for the completion of one's baptism. It is just as though two people went to the same city, and the one went by the footpath, the other by the highway, just as each thought best. So the one who binds oneself to the estate of matrimony, walks in the toils and sufferings which belong to that estate and lays upon oneself its burdens, in order that one may grow used to pleasure and sorrow, avoid sin, and prepare oneself for death better than one could do outside of that estate.

But one who seeks more suffering, and by much exercise would speedily prepare oneself for death and soon attain the goal of one's baptism, let that person be bound to chastity or to the spiritual order. For the spiritual estate, if it is as it ought to be, should be full of torment and suffering in order that one who belongs to it may have more exercise in the work of baptism than the one who is in the estate of matrimony, and through such torment quickly grow used to welcoming death with joy, and to attain the purpose of one's baptism.

Now above this estate there is yet a higher one, that which rules in the spiritual order the estate of bishop, priest, and so forth. These men should be well practiced in sufferings and works, and at every hour be ready for death—to die not only for their own sake, but also for the sake of the those who are their subjects.

Yet in all these estates, the standard, of which we spoke above, should never be forgotten, namely, that a person should so exercise oneself only to the end that sin may be driven out. One should not be driven by the number or the greatness of the works. But, alas! How we have forgotten our baptism and what it means, what vows we made there, and that we are supposed to walk in its works and to attain its purpose! So too, we have forgotten about the ways to that goal and about the estates. We hardly know to what end these estates were instituted or how we are to act in them for the fulfilling of our baptism. They have been made a sparkling show, and a little more remains of them than a worldly display. As Isaiah [1:22] says, "Your silver has become dross, your wine mixed with water." On this may God have mercy! Amen.

19. If then, the holy Sacrament of Baptism is a matter so great, gracious, and full of comfort, we should diligently see to it that we ceaselessly, joyfully, and from the heart thank, praise, and honor God for it. For I fear that by our thanklessness, we have deserved our blindness and become unworthy of recognizing such grace. The whole world was, and still is, full of baptism and the grace of God. But we have been led astray into our own anxious works, and then into indulgences and other similar false comforts. We have thought that we are not to trust God until we are righteous and have made

satisfaction for our sin, as though we would buy God's grace from God or pay God for it.

In truth, the one who does not see in God's grace how it bears with one as a sinner and will make one blessed, one who looks forward only by God's judgment, will never be joyful in God, and can neither love nor praise God. But if we hear and firmly believe that in the covenant of baptism, God receives us sinners, spares us, and makes us pure from day to day, then our heart must be joyful, and love and praise God. Thus God says through the prophet, "I will spare them as a father spares his son" [Mal 3:17]. Wherefore it is needful that we give thanks to the Blessed Majesty, who shows God's very self so gracious and merciful toward us poor condemned worms. And the work itself we must magnify and acknowledge.

THE BLESSED SACRAMENT OF THE HOLY AND TRUE BODY OF CHRIST, AND THE BROTHERHOODS

1519

1. The holy sacrament of the altar, or of the holy and true body of Christ, also has three parts, which it is necessary for us to know. The first is the sacrament, or sign. The second is the significance of this sacrament. The third is the faith required with each of the first two. These three parts must be found in every sacrament. The sacrament must be external and visible, having some material form or appearance. The significance must be internal and spiritual, within the spirit of the person. Faith must make both of them together operative and useful.

2. The sacrament, or external sign, consists in the form or appearance of bread and wine, just as baptism has water as its sign; only bread and wine must be used in eating and drinking, just as the water of baptism is used by immersion or pouring. For the sacrament, or sign, must be received, or at least desired, if it is to work a blessing. Of course, at present,

106

both kinds are not given to the people daily, as in former times. But this is not necessary since the priests partake of it daily in sight of the people. It is enough that the people desire it daily, and at present receive one kind, as the Christian Church ordains and provides.

3. For my part, however, I would consider it a good thing if the Church should again decree in general council that all persons be given both kinds, like the priests. Not because one kind is insufficient, since indeed the desire of faith is alone sufficient, as St. Augustine says, "Why do you prepare stomach and teeth? Only believe, and you have already partaken of the sacrament."[1] But it would be fitting and fine that the form, or sign, of the sacrament be given not in part only, but in its entirety, just as I said of baptism: it would be more fitting to immerse in water than to pour with it, for the sake of the completeness and perfection of the sign. For this sacrament [of the body of Christ], as we shall see, signifies the complete union and the undivided fellowship of the saints, and this is poorly and unfittingly indicated by [distributing] only one part of the sacrament. Nor is there as great a danger in the use of the cup as is supposed, since the people seldom go to this sacrament. Besides, Christ was well aware of all future dangers, and yet he saw fit to institute both kinds for the use of all his Christians.

4. The significance or effect of this sacrament is fellowship of all the saints. From this, it derives its common name *synaxis* [Greek] or *communio* [Latin], that is, fellowship. And the Latin *communicare* [commune or communicate], or as we say in German, *zum sacrament gehen* [to go to the sacrament], means to take part in the fellowship. Hence it is that Christ and all saints are one spiritual body,[2] just as the inhabitants of a city are one community and body, each citizen being a member of the other and of the entire city. All the saints, therefore, are members of Christ and of the Church, which is

a spiritual and eternal city of God.[3] And whoever is taken into this city is said to be received into the community of saints and to be incorporated into Christ's spiritual body and made a member of him. On the other hand, *excommunicare* [to excommunicate] means to put out of the community and to sever a member from this body; and that is called in our language "putting one under the ban"—though a distinction [is to be made in this regard], as I shall show in the following treatise, concerning the ban.[4]

To receive this sacrament in bread and wine, then, is nothing else than to receive a sure sign of this fellowship and incorporation with Christ and all saints. It is as if citizens were given a sign, a document, or some other token to assure them that they were citizens of the city, members of that particular community. St. Paul says this very thing in 1 Corinthians 10[:17], "We are all one bread and one body, for we all partake of one bread and of one cup." To receive this sacrament in bread and wine, then, is nothing else than to receive a sure sign of this fellowship and incorporation with Christ and all saints.

5. To carry out our homely figure, it is like a city where every citizen shares with all the others the city's name, honor, freedom, trade, customs, usages, help, support, protection, and the like, while at the same time one shares all the dangers of fire and flood, enemies and death, losses, taxes, and the like. For one who would share in the profits must also share in the costs, and ever recompense love with love. Here we see that whoever injures one citizen injures an entire city and all its citizens; whoever benefits one [citizen] deserves favor and thanks from all the others. So also in our natural body, as St. Paul says in 1 Corinthians 12[:25–26], where he gives this sacrament a spiritual explanation, "The members have [the same] care for one another, if one member suffers, all suffer together; if one member is honored, all rejoice

together." This is obvious if anyone's foot hurts, yes even the little toe, the eye looks at it at once, the fingers grasp it, the face puckers, the whole body bends over to it, and all are concerned with this small member; again, once it is cared for all the other parts are benefited. This comparison must be noted well if one wishes to understand this sacrament, for Scripture uses it for the sake of the unlearned.

6. In this sacrament, therefore, a person is given through the priest a sure sign from the very God that one is thus united with Christ and his saints and has all things in common [with them], that Christ's sufferings and life are one's own, together with the lives and sufferings of all the saints. Therefore, whoever does injury to [the believer], does injury to Christ and all the saints, as he says through the prophet [Zech 2:8], "The one who touches you touches the apple of my eye." On the other hand, whoever does a kindness to this person does it to Christ and all his saints; as he says in Matthew 25[:40], "As you did it to one of the least of these my sisters and brothers, you did it to me." Again, one must be willing to share all the burdens and misfortunes of Christ and his saints, the cost as well as the profit. Let us consider more fully these two [sides of fellowship].

7. Now adversity assails us in more than one form. There is, in the first place, the sin that remains in our flesh after baptism; the inclination to anger, hatred, pride, unchastity, and so forth. This sin assails us as long as we live. Here, we not only need the help of the community [of saints] and of Christ, in order that they might fight this sin with us, but it is also necessary that Christ and his saints intercede for us before God, so that this sin may not be charged to our account by God's strict judgment. Therefore, in order to strengthen and encourage us against this same sin, God gives us this sacrament, as much as to say, "Look, many kinds of sin are assailing you; take this sign by which I give you my

pledge that this sin is assailing not only you but also my Son, Christ, and all his saints in heaven and on earth. Therefore, take heart and be bold. You are not fighting alone. Great help and support are all around you." King David says of this bread, "The bread strengthens a person's heart" [Ps 104:15]. The Scriptures in numerous places ascribe to this sacrament the property of strengthening as in Acts 9[:18–19] [where it is written] of St. Paul, "He was baptized, and when he had received the food, he was strengthened."

In the second place, the evil spirit assails us unceasingly with many sins and afflictions. In the third place, the world, full of wickedness, entices and persecutes us and is altogether bad. Finally, our own guilty conscience assails us with our past sins; and there is the fear of death and the pains of hell. All of these afflictions make us weary and weak, unless we seek strength in this fellowship, where strength is to be found.

8. Whoever is in despair, distressed by a sin-stricken conscience or terrified by death or carrying some other burden upon their hearts, if they would be rid of them all, let them go joyfully to the sacrament of the altar and lay down their woes in the midst of the community [of saints] and seek help from the entire company of the spiritual body— just as a citizen whose property has suffered damage or misfortune at the hands of his enemies makes complaint to the town council and fellow citizens and asks them for help. The immeasurable grace and mercy of God are given us in this sacrament to the end that we might put from us all misery and tribulation [*anfechtung*] and lay it upon the community [of saints], and especially on Christ. Then we may with joy find strength and comfort, and say, "Though I am a sinner and have fallen, though this or that misfortune has befallen me, nevertheless I will go to the sacrament to receive a sign from God that I have on my side Christ's righteousness, life,

and sufferings, with all holy angels and the blessed in heaven and all pious persons on earth. If I die, I am not alone in death; if I suffer, they suffer with me. [I know that] all my misfortune is shared with Christ and the saints, because I have a sure sign of their love toward me." See, this is the benefit to be derived from this sacrament; this is the use we should make of it. The heart cannot but rejoice and be strengthened.

9. When we have shared in this sacrament, therefore, or desire to go to it, you must in turn share the misfortunes of the fellowship, as has been said. What are these? Christ in heaven and the angels together with the saints, have no misfortunes, except when injury is done to the truth and to the Word of God. Indeed, as we have said, every bane and blessing of all the saints on earth affects them. Here, your heart must go out in love and learn that this is a sacrament of love. As love and support are given you, you in turn must render love and support to Christ in his needy ones. You must feel with sorrow all the dishonor done to Christ in his holy Word, all the misery of Christendom, all the unjust suffering of the innocent, with which the world is everywhere filled to overflowing. You must fight, work, pray, and—if you cannot do more—have heartfelt sympathy. See, this is what it means to bear in your turn the misfortune and adversity of Christ and his saints. Here, the saying of Paul is fulfilled, "Bear one another's burdens, and so fulfill the law of Christ" [Gal 6:2]. See, as you uphold all of them so they all in turn uphold you; and all things are in common, both good and evil. Then all things become easy, and the evil spirt cannot stand up against this fellowship.

When Christ instituted this sacrament, he said, "This is my body which is given for you, this is my blood which is poured out for you. As often as you do this, remember me."[5] It is as if he were saying, "I am the head, I will be the first to

111

give myself for you. I will make your suffering and misfortune my own and will bear it for you, so that you in your turn may do the same for me and for one another, allowing all things to be common property, in me and with me. And I leave you this sacrament as a sure token of all this, in order that you may not forget me, but daily call to mind and admonish one another by means of what I did and am still doing for you, in order that you may be strengthened, and also bear one another in the same way."

10. This is also a reason, indeed the chief reason, why this sacrament is received many times, while baptism is received but once. Baptism is the taking up or the entering upon a new life, in the course of which boundless adversities assail us with sins and sufferings, both our own and those of others. There is the devil, the world, and our own flesh and conscience, as I have said. They never cease to hound us and oppress us. Therefore, we need the strength, support, and help of Christ and of his saints. These are pledged to us here, as in a sure sign, by which we are made one with them—incorporated into them—and all our woe is laid down in the midst of the community [of saints].

For this reason, it even happens that this holy sacrament is of little or no benefit to those who have no misfortune or anxiety, or who do not sense their adversity. It is given only to those who need strength and comfort, who have timid hearts and terrified consciences, and who are assailed by sin, or have even fallen into sin. How could it do anything for untroubled and secure spirits, who neither need nor desire it? For the Mother of God says, "He fills only the hungry [Luke 1:53], and comforts them that are distressed."

11. In order that the disciples, therefore, might by all means be worthy and well prepared for this sacrament, Christ first made them sorrowful, held before them his departure

and death, by which they became exceedingly troubled. Then he greatly terrified them when he said that one of them would betray him. When they were thus full of sorrow and anxiety, disturbed by sorrow and the sin of betrayal, then they were worthy, and he gave them his holy body to strengthen them. By which he teaches us that this sacrament is strength and comfort for those who are troubled and distressed by sin and evil. St. Augustine says the same thing, "This food demands only hungry souls, and is shunned by none so greatly as by a satisfied soul which does not need it."[6] Thus, the Jews were required to eat the Passover with bitter herbs, standing and in haste [Exod 12:8, 11]; this too signifies that this sacrament demands souls that are desirous, needy, and sorrowful. Now, if one will make the afflictions of Christ and of all Christians one's own, defend the truth, oppose unrighteousness, and help bear the needs of the innocent, and the sufferings of all Christians, then he will find affliction and adversity enough, over and above that which one's evil nature, the world, the devil, and sin daily inflict upon one. And it is even God's will and purpose to set so many hounds upon us and oppress us, and everywhere to prepare bitter herbs for us, so that we may long for this strength and take delight in the holy sacrament, and thus be worthy (that is desirous) of it.

12. It is Christ's will, then, that we partake of it frequently, in order that we may remember him and exercise ourselves in this fellowship according to his example. For if his example were no longer kept before us, the fellowship also would soon be forgotten. So we at present see to our sorrow that many Masses are held, and yet the Christian fellowship which should be preached, practiced, and kept before us by Christ's example has virtually perished. So much so that we hardly know any more what purpose this sacrament serves or how it should be used. Indeed, with our Masses, we

frequently destroy this fellowship and prevent everything. This is the fault of the preachers who do not preach the gospel or the sacraments but their humanly devised fables about the many works [of satisfaction] to be done and the ways to live right.

But in times past, this sacrament was so properly used, and the people were taught to understand this fellowship so well, that they even gathered food and material goods in the church, and there—as St. Paul writes in 1 Corinthians 11—distributed among those who were in need.[7] We have a vestige of this [practice] in the little word "collect" in the Mass, which means a general collection, just as common fund is gathered to be given to the poor. Those were the days too when so many became martyrs and saints. There were fewer Masses, but much strength and blessing resulted from the Masses; Christians cared for one another, supported one another, sympathized with one another, bore one another's burdens and affliction. This has all disappeared, and now there remain only the many Masses and the many who receive this sacrament without in the least understanding or practicing what it signifies.

13. There are those indeed, who would gladly share in the profits but not in the costs. That is, they like to hear that in this sacrament, the help, fellowship, and support of all the saints are promised and given to them. But they are unwilling in their turn to belong also to this fellowship. They will not help the poor, put up with sinners, care for the sorrowing, suffer with the suffering, intercede for others, defend the truth, and at the risk of [their own] life, property, and honor seek the betterment of the Church and of all Christians. They are unwilling because they fear the world. They do not want to have to suffer disfavor, harm, shame, or death, although it is God's will that they be so driven—for the sake of the truth and of their neighbors—to desire the great grace

and strength of this sacrament. They are self-seeking persons, whom this sacrament does not benefit. Just as we could not put up with a citizen who wanted to be helped, protected, and made free by the community, and yet in turn would do nothing for it nor serve it. No, we on our part must make the evil of others our own, if we desire Christ and his saints to make our evil their own. Then will the fellowship be complete, and justice be done to the sacrament. For the sacrament has no blessing and significance unless love grows daily and so changes a person that one made one with the others.

14. To signify this fellowship, God has appointed such signs of this sacrament as in every way serve this purpose and by their very form stimulate and motivate us to this fellowship. For just as the bread is made out of many grains, there comes the body of one bread, in which each grain loses its form and body and takes upon itself the common body of the bread; and just as the drops of wine, in losing their own form, become the body of one common wine and drink—so it is and should be with us, if we use this sacrament properly. Christ with all saints, by his love, takes upon himself our form [Phil 3:7], fights with us against sin, death, and all evil. This enkindles in us such love that we take on his form, rely upon his righteousness, life, and blessedness. And through the interchange of his blessing and our misfortunes, we become one loaf, one bread, one body, one drink, and have all things in common. O this is a great sacrament, says St. Paul, that Christ and the Church are one flesh and bone. Again, through this same love, we are to be changed and to make the infirmities of all other Christians our own; we are to take upon ourselves their form and their necessity, and all the good that is within our power we are to make theirs, that they may profit from it. That is real fellowship, and that is the true significance of this sacrament. In this way, we are

changed into one another and are made into a community by love. Without love, there can be no such change.

15. Christ appointed these two forms of bread and wine, rather than any other, as a further indication of the very union and fellowship, which is in this sacrament. For there is no more intimate, deep, and indivisible union than the union of the food with him who is fed. For the food enters into and is assimilated by his very nature and becomes one substance with the person who is fed. Other unions, achieved by such things as nails, glue, cords, and the like, do not make one indivisible substance of the objects joined together. Thus, in the sacrament, we too become united with Christ, and are made one body with all the saints, so that Christ cares for us and acts in our behalf. As if he were what we are, he makes whatever concerns us to concern him as well, and even more than it does us. In turn, we so care for Christ, as if we were what he is, which indeed we shall finally be—we shall be conformed to his likeness. As St. John says, "We know that when he shall be revealed we shall be like him" [1 John 3:2]. So deep and complete is the fellowship of Christ and all the saints with us. Thus, our sins assail him, while his righteousness protects us. For this union makes all things common, until at last Christ completely destroys sin in us and makes us like himself, at the last day. Likewise, by the same love, we are to be united with our neighbors, we in them and they in us.

16. Besides all this, Christ did not institute these two forms by themselves and alone, but he gave his true natural flesh in the bread, and his natural true blood in the wine, that he might give a really perfect sacrament or sign. For just as the bread is changed into his true natural body and the wine into his natural true blood,[8] so truly are we also drawn and changed into the spiritual body, that is, into the fellowship of Christ and all saints and by this sacrament put into

possession of all the virtues and mercies of Christ and his saints, as was said above of a citizen who is taken and incorporated into the protection and freedom of the city and the entire community. For this reason, he instituted not simply the one form, but two separate forms—his flesh under the bread, his blood under the wine—to indicate that not only his life and good works, which are indicated by his flesh and which he accomplished in his flesh, but also his passion and martyrdom, which are indicated and in which he poured out his blood, are all our own. And we, being drawn into them, may use and profit from them.

17. So it is clear from all this that this holy sacrament is nothing else than a divine sign in which are pledged, granted, and imparted Christ and all the saints together with all their works, sufferings, merits, mercies, and possessions, for the comfort and strengthening of all who are in anxiety and sorrow, persecuted by the devil, sins, the world, the flesh, and every evil. And to receive the sacrament is nothing else than to desire all this and firmly to believe that it is done.

Here, now, follows the third part of the sacrament, that is, the faith on which everything depends. For it is not enough to know what the sacrament is and signifies. It is not enough that you know it is a fellowship and a gracious exchange or blending of our sin and suffering with the righteousness of Christ and his saints. You must also desire it and firmly believe that you have received it. Here, the devil and our own nature wage their fiercest fight, so that faith may by no means stand firm. There are those who practice their arts and subtleties by trying [to fathom] what becomes of the bread when it is changed into Christ's flesh and of the wine when it is changed into his blood and how the whole Christ, his flesh and blood, can be encompassed in so small a portion of bread and wine. It does not matter if you do not see it. It is enough to know that it is a divine sign in which Christ's flesh and blood are truly present. The how and the where we leave to him.

18. See to it that here you exercise and strengthen your faith, so that when you are sorrowful or when your sins press you and you go to the sacrament or hear Mass, you do so with a hearty desire for this sacrament and for what it signifies. Then do not doubt that you have what the sacrament signifies, that is, be certain that Christ and all his saints are coming to you with all their virtues, sufferings, and mercies, to live, work, suffer, and die with you, and that they desire to be wholly yours, having all these things in common with you. If you will exercise and strengthen this faith, then you will experience what a rich, joyous, and beautiful wedding feast your God has prepared for you upon the altar. Then you will understand what the great feast of King Ahasuerus signifies [Esth 1:5]; and you will see what that wedding feast is for which God slew his oxen and fat calves, as it is written in the Gospel [Matt 22:2–4]. Then your heart will become truly free and confident, strong and courageous against all enemies [Ps 23:5]. For who will fear any calamity if one is sure that Christ and all his saints are with one and have all things, evil or good, in common with one? So we read in Acts 2[:46] that the disciples of Christ broke this bread and ate with great gladness of heart. Since, there, this work is so great that the smallness of our souls would not dare to desire it, to say nothing of hoping for it or expecting it, therefore it is necessary and profitable to go often to the sacrament, or at least in the daily Mass to exercise and strengthen this faith on which the whole thing depends and for the sake of which it was instituted. For if you doubt, you do God the greatest dishonor and make him out to be a faithless liar; if you cannot believe, then pray for faith, as was said earlier in the other treatise.[9]

19. See to it also that you give yourself to everyone in fellowship and by no means exclude anyone in hatred or

anger. For this sacrament of fellowship, love, and unity cannot tolerate discord and disunity. You must take to heart the infirmities and needs of others, as if they were your own. Then offer to others your strength, as if it were their own, just as Christ does for you in the sacrament. This is what it means to be changed into one another through love, out of many particles to become one bread and drink, to lose one's own form and take on that which is common to all.

For this reason, slanderers and those who wickedly judge and despise others cannot but receive death in the sacrament, as St. Paul writes in 1 Corinthians 11 [:29]. For they do not do for their neighbor what they seek from Christ, and what the sacrament indicates. They begrudge others anything good; they have no sympathy for them; they do not care for others as they themselves desire to be cared for by Christ. And then they fall into such blindness that they do not know what else to do in this sacrament except to fear and honor Christ, there present with their own prayers and devotion. When they have done this, they think they have done their whole duty. But Christ has given his holy body for this purpose, that the thing signified by the sacrament—the fellowship, the change wrought by love—may be put into practice. And Christ values his spiritual body, which is the fellowship of his saints, more than his own natural body. To him, it is more important, especially in this sacrament, that faith in the fellowship with him and with his saints may be properly exercised and become strong in us; and that we, in keeping with it, may properly exercise our fellowship with one another. This purpose of Christ, the blind worshippers do not perceive. In their devoutness, they go on daily saying and hearing Mass, but they remain every day the same; indeed, every day they become worse but do not perceive it.

Therefore, take heed. It is more needful that you discern the spiritual than the natural body of Christ; and faith in the spiritual body is more necessary than faith in the natural body. For the natural without the spiritual profits us nothing in this sacrament; a change must occur [in the communicant] and be exercised through love.

20. There are many who, regardless of this change of love and faith, rely upon the fact that the Mass or the sacrament is, as they say *opus gratum opere operato*, that is, a work which of itself pleases God, even though they who perform it do not please God. From this, they conclude that however unworthily Masses are said, it is nonetheless a good thing to have many Masses, since harm comes [only] to those who say or use them unworthily. I grant everyone [the right to] one's opinion, but such fables do not please me. For, [if you desire] to speak in these terms, there is no creature or work that does not of itself please God, as is written in Genesis 1 [:31], "God saw all of God's works and indeed, it was very good." What is the result if bread, wine, gold, and all good things are misused, even though of themselves they are pleasing to God? Why, the consequence of that is condemnation. So also here the more precious the sacrament, the greater the harm which comes upon the whole community [of saints] from its misuse. For it was not instituted for its own sake, that it might please God, but for our sake, that we might use it right, exercise our faith by it, and through it become pleasing to God. If it is merely an *opus operatum*,[10] it works only harm everywhere; it must become an *opus operantis*.[11] Just as bread and wine, no matter how much they may please God in and of themselves, work only harm if they are not used, so it is not enough that the sacrament be merely completed (that is, *opus operatum*); it must also be used in faith (that is, *opus operantis*). And we must take care lest with such dangerous interpretations the sacrament's power and virtue be lost on us, and faith perish utterly through the false security of the [outwardly] completed sacrament.

All this comes from the fact that they pay more attention in this sacrament to Christ's natural body than to the fellowship, the spiritual body. Christ on the cross was also a completed work which was well pleasing to God. But to this day, the Jews have found it a stumbling block because they did not construe it as a work that is made use of in faith. See to it, then, that for you, the sacrament is an *opus operantis*, that is, a work that is made use of, that is well pleasing to God not because of what it is in in itself but because of your faith and your good use of it. The Word of God too is of itself pleasing to God, but it is harmful to me unless in me it also pleases God. In short, such expressions as *opus operatum* and *opus operantis* are vain words that are more of a hindrance than a help. And who could tell of all the abominable abuses and misbeliefs which daily multiply about this blessed sacrament, some of which are so spiritual and holy that they might almost lead an angel astray?

Briefly, whoever would understand the abuses need only keep in mind what has already been said about the use and faith of this sacrament; namely, that there must be a sorrowing, hungry soul, who desires heartily the love, help, and support of the entire community—of Christ and of all Christendom—and who does not doubt that in faith [all these desires] are obtained, and who makes oneself one with everyone. Whoever does not take this as the point of departure for arranging and ordering one's hearing or reading of Masses and one's receiving of the sacrament is in error and does not use this sacrament to one's salvation. It is for this reason also that the world is overrun with pestilences, wars, and other horrible plagues,[12] because with our many Masses we only bring down upon us greater disfavor.

21. We see now how necessary this sacrament is for those who must face death, or other dangers of body and soul, that they not be left to them alone but be strengthened

in the fellowship of Christ and all saints. This is why Christ instituted it and gave it to his disciples in the hour of their extreme need and peril. Since we then are all daily surrounded by all kinds of danger, and must at last die, we should humbly and heartily give thanks with all our powers to the God of all mercy for giving us such a gracious sign, by which—if we hold fast to it in faith—God leads and draws us through death and every danger unto Godself, unto Christ and all saints.

Therefore, it is also profitable and necessary that the love and fellowship of Christ and all saints be hidden, invisible, and spiritual, and that only a bodily, visible, and outward sign of it be given to us. For if this love, fellowship, and support were apparent to all, like the transient fellowship of people, we would not be strengthened or trained by it to desire or put our trust in the things that are unseen and eternal [2 Cor 4:18]. Instead, we would be trained to put our trust only in things that are transient and seen, and would become so accustomed to them as to be unwilling to let them go; we would not follow God, except so far as visible and tangible things led us. In this way, we would be prevented from ever coming to God. For everything that is bound to time and sense must fall away, and we must learn to do without them, if we are to come to God.

For this reason the Mass and this sacrament are a sign by which we train and accustom ourselves to let go of all visible love, help, and comfort, and to trust in the invisible love, help, and support of Christ and his saints. For death takes away all the things that are seen and separates us from people and transcendent things. To meet it, we must, therefore, have the help of the things that are unseen and eternal. And these are indicated to us in the sacrament and sign, to which we cling by faith until we finally attain to them also with sight and senses.

Thus, the sacrament is for us a ford, a bridge, a door, a ship, and a stretcher, by which and in which we pass from this world into eternal life. Therefore, everything depends on faith. He who does not believe is like the person who is supposed to cross the sea, who is so timid that one does not trust the ship; and so one must remain and never be saved, because that one will not embark and cross over. This is the fruit which shrinks from the passage across the Jordan of death, and the devil too has a generous hand in it.

22. This was signified long ago in Joshua 3[:14–17]. After the children of Israel had gone dry-shod through the Red Sea [Exod 14:21–22]—in which [event] baptism was typified—they went through the Jordan also in like manner. But the priests stood with the ark in the Jordan, and the water below them was cut off, while the water above them rose up like a mountain—in which [event] this sacrament is typified. The priests hold and carry the ark in the Jordan when, in the hour of our death or peril, they preach and administer to us this sacrament, the fellowship of Christ and all the saints. If we then believe, the waters below us depart, that is, the things that are seen and transient do nothing but flee from us. The waters above us, however, well up high; that is, the horrible torments of the other world, which we envision at the hour of death, terrify us as if they would overwhelm us. If, however, we pay no attention to them, and walk over with a firm faith, then we shall enter dry-shod and unharmed into eternal life.

We have, therefore, two principal sacraments in the Church, baptism and the bread. Baptism leads us into a new life on earth; the bread guides us through death into eternal life. And the two are signified by the Red Sea and the Jordan, and by the two lands, one beyond and one on this side of the Jordan. This is why our Lord said of the Last Supper, "I shall not drink again of this wine until I drink it new with you in my Father's kingdom" [Matt 26:29]. So entirely is this sacrament intended and instituted for a strengthening against death and an entrance into eternal life.

In conclusion, the blessing of this sacrament is fellowship and love, by which we are strengthened against death and all evil. This fellowship is twofold: on the one hand, we partake of Christ and all saints; on the other hand, we permit all Christians to be partakers of us, in whatever way they are and we are able. Thus, by means of this sacrament, all self-seeking love is rooted out and gives place to that which seeks the common good of all; and through the change brought about by love, there is one bread, one drink, one body, one community. This is the true unity of Christian community.

THE CONFESSION CONCERNING CHRIST'S SUPPER

1528

MY GROUNDS, on which I rest in this matter, are as follows: The first is this article of our faith, that Jesus Christ is essential, natural, true, complete God and human in one person, undivided and inseparable. The second, that the right hand of God is everywhere. The third, that the Word of God is not false or deceitful. The fourth, that God has and knows various ways to be present at a certain place, not only the single one of which the fanatics prattle, which the philosophers call "local." Of this, the sophists[1] properly say: There are three modes of being present in a given place: locally or circumscriptively, definitively, repletively.

Let me translate this for the sake of clearer understanding. In the first place, an object is circumscriptively or locally in a place, i.e., in a circumscribed manner,[2] if the space and the object occupying it exactly correspond and fit into the same measurements, such as wine or water in a cask, where the wine occupies no more space and the cask yields no more space than the volume of the wine. Or, a piece of wood or a tree in the water takes up no more space, and the water yields no more, than the size of the tree in it. Again, a person walking in the open air takes up no more space from the air around that person, nor does the air yield more, than the size of the person. In this mode, space and object correspond exactly, item by item, just as a pewterer measures, pours off, and molds the tankard in its form.

In the second place, an object is in a place definitively, i.e., in an uncircumscribed manner, if the object or body is not palpably in one place and is not measurable according to the dimensions of the place where it is, but can occupy either more room or less. Thus it is said that angels and spirits are in certain places. For an angel or devil can be present in an entire house or city; again, they can be in a room, a chest, or a box, indeed, in a nutshell. The space is really material and circumscribed, and has its own dimensions of length, breadth, and depth; but that which occupies it has not the same length, breadth, or depth as the space which it occupies. Indeed, it has no length or breadth at all. Thus, we read in the Gospel that the devil possesses persons and enters them, and they also enter into swine. Indeed, in Matthew 8[:28ff.] we read that a whole legion was in one man. That would be about six thousand devils. This I call an uncircumscribed presence in a given place, since we cannot circumscribe or measure it as we measure a body, and yet it is obviously present in the place.

This was the mode in which the body of Christ was present when he came out of the closed grave and came to the disciples through a closed door as the Gospels show.[3] There was no measuring or defining of the space his head or foot occupied when he passed through the stone, yet he certainly had to pass through it. He took up no space, and the stone yielded him no space, but the stone remained stone, as entire and firm as before, and his body remained as large and thick as it was before. But he also was able, when he wished, to let himself be seen circumscribed in given places where he occupied space and his size could be measured. Just so, Christ can be and is in the bread, even though he can also show himself in circumscribed and visible form wherever he wills. For as the sealed stone and the closed door remained unaltered and unchanged, though his body at the same time was in the space, entirely occupied by stone and wood, so he is also at the same time in the sacrament and where the bread and wine are, though the bread and wine in themselves remain unaltered and unchanged.

In the third place, an object occupies places repletively, i.e., supernaturally, it is simultaneously present in all places whole and entire, and fills all places, yet without being measured or circumscribed by any place, in terms of the space which it occupies. This mode of existence belongs to God alone, as it says in the prophet Jeremiah [23:23f.], "I am a God at hand and not afar off. I fill heaven and earth." This mode is altogether incomprehensible, beyond our reason, and can be maintained only with faith, in the Word.

All this I have related in order to show that there are more modes by which an object may exist in a place than the one circumscribed, physical mode on which the fanatics insist. Moreover, Scripture irresistibly forces us to believe that Christ's body does not have to be present in a given place circumscriptively or corporeally, occupying and filling space in proportion to its size. For it was in the stone at the grave, but not in that circumscribed mode; similarly, in the closed door, as they cannot deny. If it could be present there without space and place proportionate to its size, my friend, why can't it also be in the bread without space and room proportionate to its size? But if it can be present in this uncircumscribed manner, it is beyond the realm of material creatures and it is not grasped or measured in these terms. Who can know how this takes place? Who will prove it false if someone declares that, since Christ's body is outside the realm of creation, it can assuredly be wherever he wishes, and that all creatures are as permeable and present to him as another body's material place or location is to it?

Consider our physical eyes and our power of vision. When we open our eyes, in one moment our sight is five or six miles away, and simultaneously present everywhere within the range of those six miles. Yet, this is only a matter of sight, the power of the eye. If the physical sight can do this, do you not think that God's power can also find a way by which all creatures can be present and permeable to Christ's body? "Yes," you may say, "but by this you do not prove that it is so." Thank you, I prove this much by it: that the fanatics also cannot refute me and prove that this is impossible to the divine power, which they should and must do. That should prove, I say, that God knows no other way by which the body of Christ can exist in a given place than corporeally and circumscriptively. If they cannot do this, their system stands disgraced. Of course, they cannot do it.

Because we prove from Scripture, however, that Christ's body can exist in a given place in other modes than this corporeal one, we have by the same token sufficiently argued that the words, "This is my body," ought to be believed as they read. For it is contrary to no article of faith, and moreover it is scriptural, in that Christ's body is held to have passed through the sealed stone and the closed door. Since we can point out a mode of existence other than the corporeal, circumscribed one, who will be so bold as to measure and span the power of God, as if God knows of no other modes? Yet the position of the fanatics cannot be maintained unless they can prove that the power of God can be measured and spanned in this way, for their whole argument rests on the assertion that the body of Christ can exist in a given place only in a corporeal and circumscribed manner.

But here they are not answering but leaping over the question while they chatter about Lady Alloeosis.[4]

And now to come to my own position. Our faith maintains that Christ is God and human, and the two natures are one person, so that this person may not be divided in two; therefore, God can surely reveal God's very self in a corporeal, circumscribed manner at whatever place God wills, as God did after the resurrection and will do on the last day. But above and beyond this mode, God can also use the second, uncircumscribed mode, as we have proven from the Gospel that he did at the grave and the closed door.

But now, since he is a man who is supernaturally one person with God, and apart from this man there is no God, it must follow that according to the third supernatural mode, he is and can be wherever God is, and that everything is full of Christ through and through, even according to his humanity—not according to the first corporeal, circumscribed mode, but according to the supernatural, divine mode. Here you must take your stand and say that wherever Christ is according to his divinity, he is there as a natural divine person, and he is also naturally and personally there, as his conception in his mother's womb proves conclusively. For if he was the Son of God, he had to be in his mother's womb naturally and personally wherever he is, then he must be man there, too, since he is not two separate persons but a single person. Wherever this person is, it is the single, indivisible person, and if you can say, "Here is God," then you must also say, "Christ the man is present too."

And if you could show me one place where God is and not the man, then the person is already divided and I could at once say truthfully, "Here is God who is not human and has never become human." But no God like that for me! For it would follow from this that space and place had separated the two natures from one another and in this way had divided the person, even though death and all the devils had been unable to separate and tear them apart. This would leave me a poor sort of Christ, if he were present only in one single place, as a divine and human person, and if at all other places he had to be nothing more than a mere isolated God and a divine person without the humanity. No, comrade, wherever you place God for me, you must also place the humanity for me. They simply will not let themselves be separated and divided from each other. He has become one person and does not separate the humanity from himself as Master Jack takes off his coat and lays it aside when he goes to bed.

Let me give a simple illustration for the common person. The humanity is more closely united with God than our skin with our flesh—yes, more closely than body and soul. Now, as long as a person lives and remains in health, one's skin and flesh, body and soul are so completely one being, one person, that they cannot be separated; on the contrary, wherever the soul is, there must the body be also, and wherever the flesh is, there must the skin be also. You cannot indicate a special place or space where the soul is present alone without the body, like a kernel without the shell, or where the flesh is without the skin, like a pea without a pod. On the contrary, wherever the one is, there must the other be also. Thus you cannot shell the divinity from the humanity and lay it aside at some place away from the humanity. For in this way, you would be dividing the person and making the humanity merely a pod, indeed a coat, which the divinity put on and off according to the availability of place and space. Thus the physical space would have the power to divide the person, although neither angels nor all creation can do so.

Here you will say with Nicodemus, "How can this be?" [John 3:9]. Must all places and space now become one space and place? Or, as a dolt dreams according to a crude and fleshly sense, must the humanity of Christ stretch and extend itself like a skin as wide as all creation? I answer: here you must with Moses take off your old shoes, and with Nicodemus be born anew.[5] According to your old notion, which perceives no more than the first, corporeal, circumscribed mode, you will understand this as little as the fanatics, who cannot think of the Godhead in any other way than existing everywhere in a corporeal, circumscribed mode, as if God were some vast, extended entity that pervades and embraces all creation. Thus, you may gather from their charge that we stretch and extend the humanity and in this way enclose the divinity. Such words obviously apply to the corporeal, circumscribed mode of being, as a peasant stuffs himself into his jacket and trousers, when the jacket and trousers are expanded so that they will go around his body and his legs....

Christ says, "If I have told you earthly things and you do not believe me, how can you believe it if I tell you heavenly things?" [John 3:12]. Behold, this is entirely an earthly and bodily thing when Christ's body passes through the stone and the door. For his body is an object which can be laid hold of, as much so as the stone and the door. Still, no reason can grasp how his body and the stone are in one place at the same time when he passes through it, and yet neither does the stone become larger or expand more, nor Christ's body smaller or more compressed. Here, faith must blind reason and lift out of the physical, circumscribed mode into the second uncircumscribed mode, which it does not understand but cannot deny.

Now, if the second mode must be understood by faith, and reason with its first circumscribed mode must vanish, how much more must faith alone remain here and reason vanish in the case of the heavenly, supernatural mode, where Christ's body is one person with God in the Godhead? For everyone will grant me this, that it is a far different and higher mode when Christ's body is in the sealed stone and the closed door, than when according to the first mode, it sits or stands in his clothes or walks in the open air about him. For here the air and the clothes extend and stretch themselves according to the size of his body, which the eyes can see and the hands can touch. But in the stone and the door there is no expansion.

Further, everyone will grant me that it is a far more exalted existence and mode when Christ's body is one person with God, than when it is in the stone or the door. For God is no corporeal thing but a Spirit above all things. And Christ is not one person with the stone or the door, as he is with God. Therefore, he must be in the Godhead in a greater and more profound manner than he is in the stone or the door, just as he is in the stone and the door more intimately and profoundly than in his clothes or in the open air. And if the stone and the door did not have to extend or expand themselves, nor enclose the body of Christ, much less in this most exalted mode does the humanity extend and expand itself or enclose and compress the divinity, as this fleshly spirit dreams.

The spirit must answer me and acknowledge that Christ's body has a far higher, supernatural existence, since he is one person with God, than he had when he was in the sealed stone and the door, since this is the highest mode and existence there is, and there cannot be anything higher than for a person to be one with God. For the second mode, in which Christ's body existed in the stone, will also be common to all the saints in heaven; they will pass with their bodies through all the objects of creation, a property which is common even now to angels and devils. For the angel came to Peter in the prison, Acts 12[:7]. And goblins come daily into closed chambers and storerooms. So he must also grant me that the stone does not extend itself or enclose Christ's body....[6]

Thus the one body of Christ has a threefold existence, or all three modes of being at a given place. First, the circumscribed corporeal mode of presence, as when he walked bodily on earth, as when he occupied and yielded space according to his size. He can still employ this mode of presence when he wills to do so, as he did after his resurrection and as he will do on the last day, as Paul says in 1 Timothy [6:15], "Whom the blessed God will reveal," and Colossians 3[:4], "When Christ your life reveals himself." He is not in God or with the Father in heaven according to this mode, as this mad spirit dreams, for God is not a corporeal space or place. The passage which the spiritualists adduce concerning Christ's leaving the world and going to the Father[7] speak of this mode of presence.

Secondly, the uncircumscribed, spiritual mode of presence according to which he neither occupies nor yields space but passes through everything created as he wills. To use some crude illustration, my vision passes through and exists in air, light, or water and does not occupy or yield any space; a sound or tone passes through and exists in air or water or a board and a wall and neither occupies nor yields space; likewise, light and heat go through and exist in air, water, glass, or crystals and the like, but without occupying or yielding space, and many more like these. He employed this mode of presence when he left the closed grave and came through closed doors, in the bread and wine in the Supper, and as people believe, when he was born in his mother.

Thirdly, since he is one person with God, the divine, heavenly mode, according to which all created things are indeed much more permeable and present to him than they are according to the second mode. For if according to the second mode he can be present in and with created things in such a way that they do not feel, touch, measure, or circumscribe him, how much more marvelously will he be present in all created things according to this exalted third mode, where they cannot measure or circumscribe him but where they are present to him so that he measures and circumscribes them. You must place this existence of Christ, which constitutes him one person with God, far, far beyond things created, as far as God transcends them; and, on the other hand, place it as deep in and as near to all created things as God is in them. For God, he is one indivisible person with God, and wherever God is, he must be also, otherwise our faith is false.

But who can explain or even conceive how this occurs? We know indeed that it is so, that he is in God beyond all created things, and is one person with God. But how this happens, we do not know; it transcends nature and reason, even the comprehension of all the angels in heaven, and is known only to God. Since this is true, even though unknown to us, we should not give the lie to his words until we know how to prove certainly that the body of Christ cannot in any circumstances be where God is and this mode of being is fiction....

See then, what a beautiful, great, marvelous thing this is, how everything meshes together in one sacramental reality. The words are the first thing, for without the words, the cup, the body and blood of Christ, would not be there. Without the body and blood of Christ, the new testament would not be there. Without the new testament, forgiveness of sins would not be there. Without forgiveness of sins, life and salvation would not be there. Thus the words first connect the bread and cup to the sacrament; bread and cup embrace the body and blood of Christ; body and blood of Christ embrace the new testament; the new testament embraces the forgiveness of sins; forgiveness of sins embraces eternal life and salvation. See, all this the words of the Supper offer and give us, and we embrace it by faith.

A SERMON ON PREPARING TO DIE

Martin Luther, Augustinian

FIRST, BECAUSE death means saying goodbye to this world and all its activities, it is necessary for a person to arrange one's earthly possessions appropriately, thinking to order them in such a way that after one's death, no cause is left for conflict, quarrels, or other misunderstandings among the remaining relatives and friends. This pertains to the bodily and external farewell to this world and leaving behind our possessions.

Next, one should also take leave spiritually, that is, to forgive, in only a friendly way, all those who have harmed us, alone for God's sake. On the other hand, also for God's sake, ask to be forgiven by all those whom we have no doubt harmed, at least by setting a bad example or by helping too little with good deeds that we owed them, according to the command of Christian brotherly and sisterly love. Sharing forgiveness in this way is necessary so that the soul does not remain arrested in any affairs on earth.

Thirdly, after one has taken leave from everyone on earth, one should orient oneself toward God, to whom the path of death itself guides and directs us. This is where the narrow gate[1] and the small, straight path to life begin. Everyone will have to venture out joyfully on this path, which, although very narrow, is not long. What takes place here is just like the birth of an infant. With peril, pain, and fear it comes out of the small abode of its mother's womb into an immense heaven and earth, that is, into this world. In the same way, the person goes through the narrow gate of death, out of this life. And although we perceive the heavens and the world in which we now dwell as great and wide, they are narrower and smaller by far than our mother's womb as compared with the future heaven. Therefore, the death of the dear saints is called a new birth, and their feast day in Latin is called *Natale*,[2] the day of their birth. The narrow passageway of death, however, makes us take this life to be expansive and the life beyond to be confined. Therefore, one has to believe and learn the lesson from the physical birth of a child, the way Christ says, "When a woman is in labor, she has sorrow, but when she has recovered, she no longer remembers her anguish, because of the joy of having brought a human being into the world."[3] So in dying one must also endure the pain and anguish and know that a spacious mansion and joy await us.

Fourthly, in order to prepare and become ready for this journey, one must undertake a sincere confession (of at least the greatest sins and those that, by diligently searching, one can recall into memory), and one must yearn reverently for the holy Christian sacrament of the holy and true body of Christ, and extreme unction (or last rites), receiving them with confident expectations, if they are available. When they are not, then your yearning and wanting them should console you at least as much as receiving them. Do not be frightened too much if you do not receive them. Christ says, "All things are possible for the one who believes."[4] Because the sacraments are nothing more than signs that serve and stimulate our faith, as we shall see. And without such faith, they have no value.

Fifthly, one must earnestly and diligently take care to see the sacraments as momentous, hold them in honor, relying freely and joyfully on them, and weighing them in the balance in order by far to outstrip sin, death, and hell. We should also occupy ourselves more with the sacraments and their virtues than our sins. We have to know how to honor them properly and know their virtues. I show them their proper honor when I believe that I truly receive what the sacraments signify, along with all that God declares and indicates in them, so that I can say with Mary, the Mother of God, in steadfast faith, "Let it be to me according to your words and signs."[5] Since God's very self here speaks and acts through the priest, one could not dishonor God's Word and work more than by doubting its truth. And we can do no greater honor than to believe God's Word and work are true by freely relying on them.

Sixthly, to know the virtues[6] of the sacraments, we must know the evils that they contend with and that we face. There are three such evils: first, the very frightening image of death; next, the gruesome manifold image of sin; and third, the unbearable and unavoidable image of hell and eternal damnation. Every other evil ensues from these three, which magnify in strength as a result of their mutual reinforcement.

Death looms so large and frightening because our weak and fainthearted nature has etched that image too vividly within itself and constantly fixes its gaze on it. In addition, the devil presses the person to look closely at the mien and image of death to increase worry, timidity, and despair. Indeed, the devil conjures up before the person's eyes all kinds of sudden and frightening deaths, those ever seen, heard, or read about by people. Then the evil one slyly reminds of the wrath of God, by which in earlier days and at various times the devil tormented and destroyed sinners. In that way, he fills our weak human nature with the dread of death, while cultivating a love and concern for life, so that the person becomes overly burdened by such thoughts, forgetting God, fleeing and abhorring death, and thus finally becoming and remaining disobedient to God. Because the deeper we contemplate, view, and get to know death, the more difficult and dangerous it is to die. We should familiarize ourselves with death during our lifetime, inviting death into our presence when it is still at a distance and not on the move. At the time of dying, bringing up death is hazardous and useless, for death already looms large on its own account. In that hour, we must put the thought of death out of our mind and refuse to see it, as we shall hear. The power and strength of death are rooted in the fearfulness of our nature and in our untimely and undue viewing and contemplating of it.

Seventhly, sin magnifies and grows ominous when we dwell on it and brood over it too much. This is increased by the fearfulness of our conscience, which feels ashamed before God and punishes itself grimly. That is where the devil has looked for and found a real hot tub of sin to drive us and soak us in, to increase and multiply them. Then before a person's eyes, he can display all kinds of sinners, especially those who were condemned for sins not even as great as one's own. In this way, the evil one makes the person despair and reluctant to die, thus forgetting God and becoming disobedient even in the hour of death. This is true especially because the person thinks it is appropriate to contemplate one's sins and that one does right when concerned about one's sins at this time. With that one finds oneself unprepared and unfit to such a degree that even all one's good works are turned into sins. The result has to be an unwillingness to die, disobedience to the will of God, and eternal damnation. This is not the fitting time to meditate on one's sin. One should do that during one's lifetime. This is the way the evil spirit distorts all things. It's during our lives that we should let sin, death, and hell continually come before our eyes, the way we read in the Psalm, "My sin is ever before me."[7] During our lives, the devil closes our eyes and hides this image. But at death, when we should only have life, grace, and salvation before our eyes, then for the first time, he opens our eyes and frightens us with this untimely image, in order that we do not see the appropriate images.

Eighthly, hell also looms up and mushrooms when we consider it and brood about it at the wrong time. This is exacerbated to a measureless degree by our ignorance of God's counsel. The evil spirit prods the soul so that it burdens itself with all kinds of useless presumptions, especially with the most dangerous undertaking of delving into the mystery of God's will to ascertain whether one is "predestined" or "chosen" or not. This is where the devil exercises his last and most treacherous art and capability. Because with that he leads the person (before one knows it) above God, so that one looks for a sign from God's will and becomes impatient that one should not know if one is predestined or not. It makes one suspicious of God, so that one very nearly looks for a different god. In short, at this point, the devil thinks to extinguish the love of God in a storm and awaken a hatred for God. The more the person follows the devil and allows these thoughts, the more dangerous they get, so that finally one cannot withstand blasphemy and hatred for God. For what else is it to want to know if I am predestined than to want to know everything God knows and be equal to God? So that God does not know more than I? Thus I do not let God be God, who should not know any more than what I know. Then, before our eyes, the devil presents to us many heathen, Jews, and Christian children that have become lost, compelling so many of such dangerous and presupposed thoughts, that the person who would otherwise have gladly died, because of this part, now becomes unwilling to die. This is what it is to be threatened by hell: when a person is confronted with thoughts about one's predestination, about which there are many complaints in the Psalms. Whoever wins at this point has overcome hell, sin, and death together.

Ninthly, in these activities, one must with diligence turn away from inviting these three images into your home, not paint the devil on your door, because he will break in through it strongly enough by himself and dispute, argue, and occupy your heart with these images.[8] When this happens, the person is lost and forgets God completely, because these images do not at all belong in your mind at this time, except to fight with them and drive them away. Where the images stand alone, they do not belong anywhere but in hell, under the devil. One must see through them to grace, life, and heaven.

Now, whoever wants to fight with them, it will not be enough to scuffle, struggle, bat, and wrestle against them, because they will be too strong for you and things will get worse and worse. The real art and skill is just to let them fall completely away and have nothing to do with them. How does that work? It works like this: you should not allow yourself to be driven by them from your looking and seeing life in death, grace in sin, and heaven in hell, even if all the angels and creatures, yes, even if you think God's very self, try to divert you from that view, which they do not; but the evil spirit gives this false impression. What can one do?

Tenthly, you should not view or consider death in itself—not in yourself, your nature, nor in the ones killed by God's wrath and overcome by death—otherwise, you are lost and with it you will be overcome. But turn your eyes away—and the thoughts of your heart and all your being—from this image of death and look at those intensely and diligently who have died in God's grace and who have overcome death, preeminently Christ and, after him, all the saints. Viewing these images themselves, death will not be terrifying and gruesome for you, but even hatefully disregarded, killed, choked to death, and overcome by life. For Christ is nothing other than sheer life, and his saints too; the deeper and more firmly that you engrave their image in yourself, seeing them, the more the image of death will fall away and disappear by itself, without the strain of fighting and struggle. With that, your heart will have peace and you can die peacefully in and with Christ. As written in Revelation, "Blessed are those who die in the lord Christ."[9] That is also the meaning of Numbers, chapter 21, where the children of Israel were bitten by snakes. They did not strain and struggle, fighting with those snakes, but they had to gaze at the dead, bronze serpent, and with that, the living snakes fell off them by themselves and left them. Thus, you have to concern yourself with the death of Christ alone so that you will find life, because, if you look at death any other way, it will kill you with extreme anguish and suffering. That is why Jesus says, "In the world (that is, also in ourselves) we will have troubles, but in me, you will have peace."[10]

Eleventh, therefore, you should not look at sin in sinners, in your own conscience, or in those who remain in sin until they die and are condemned; for if you do, you will certainly take a back seat and be driven to destruction by them. But turn away from those thoughts and view your sin only within the image of grace, and engrave that image within yourself, and with all your strength, keep that image before your eyes. The image of grace is nothing other than Christ on the cross and all his dear saints. How can one understand this? It is the grace and mercy of Christ on the cross taking all your sins away from you, bearing them for you, and strangling them.

Believe that firmly and fix it before your eyes without doubting it. That is what is called gazing at the image of grace and engraving it in yourself. This is the same thing all the saints have done in their suffering and dying. They also take all your sins upon themselves and suffer and labor for you, as it is written, "Bear one another's burdens and in that you will fulfill the law of Christ."[11] And in Matthew, Jesus himself says, "Come unto me all you who labor, are weary and heavy laden, I will help you.[12] You can look at your sin in this way safely without tormenting your conscience. Look, now your sins are no longer sins anymore, they have been overcome and swallowed up in Christ. For the same way that Christ takes your death upon himself and strangles it so that it cannot harm you, when you believe that he does that for you and you see your death in him and not in yourself, that is also the same way that Christ takes your sin upon himself, and through sheer grace, in his righteousness overcomes your sin. When you believe it, your sins will never harm you. That is the way Christ, our comfort, is the image of life and grace against the image of death and sin, so that Paul says, "Thanks and praise be to God, who through Christ gives us the victory over sin and death!"[13]

Twelfth, you must not gaze at hell and the eternity of pain in relation to predestination—not in you, not in itself, and not in those who are damned. And do not concern yourself with how many people the whole world over are not chosen, because if you are not careful, that image [in your mind] can quickly become your downfall and knock you to the ground. Therefore, you have to use force and shut your eyes tightly and not take that look, because it is completely useless. Even if you concerned yourself with it for a thousand years and destroyed yourself with it to boot, you will still have to let God be God and [realize] that God knows more about you than you know about yourself. That is the reason for the heavenly image of Christ, who for your sake descended into hell[14] and was forsaken by God like one who was damned by God forever, even as he says from the cross: "*Eli, Eli, lama sabachthani?*" "My God, my God, why have you forsaken me?"[15] Look, in that image, you have the victory over hell and in it your uncertain predestination is made certain; for, if you concern yourself with that image alone and believe it took place for you, then you will certainly be kept in that faith. Therefore, just do not let it be removed from your eyes and seek yourself only in Christ and not in yourself and then you will find yourself in him eternally.

Thus, when you gaze at Christ and all his saints and you are well pleased by the grace of God, who also chose them, and you yourself remain steadfast in that joy, then you are also chosen, as God says in Genesis, "All who bless you shall be blessed."[16] But if you do not cling to this alone and you fall into yourself, then displeasure will awaken in yourself against God and the saints, and then you will find nothing good in yourself. Beware of that, because the evil spirit, with many cunning deceptions, can drive you to such a pass.

Thirteenth, these three images or conflicts are foreshadowed in Judges, where Gideon attacks the Midianites with three hundred men in three places at night. He did no more than allow trumpets to be blown and glass jars and lanterns to be smashed; with that, the enemy fled and strangled themselves. In that same way, death, sin, hell, and all their forces flee when we practice only having the glowing image of Christ and his saints before us in the night, that is, in faith, which does not see, nor want to see, the evil image. In addition, they incite and strengthen us with God's Word as if by the sound of trumpets. Isaiah leads us with the same figure of speech,[17] a rather lovely one against the same threesome image and it speaks about Christ, "The weight of his burden and the scourge of his back, and the rod of his oppressors, you have overcome just like in the times of Midian," who were overcome by Gideon,[18] as if the prophet was speaking of your people's sin (that is, the heavy weight burdening the conscience), death (that is, the scourge or punishment which presses upon one's back), and hell (that is, the rod and violence of the oppressor that is required to pay eternally for sin). If you have overcome it all, like happened in the time of Midian, then it is also through faith, for Gideon drove the enemy to flight without wielding the sword.

When did Christ do this? On the cross! Because it is there that Christ prepared himself to be the threefold image, to behold before the eyes of our faith against the three images with which the evil spirit and our nature attack us in order to rip us out of our faith. Christ is the living and undying image against the death that he had suffered. With his resurrection from the dead, however, he conquered suffering and death in his life. He is the image of the grace of God against sin, which he took upon himself and overcame by his invincible obedience. Christ is the heavenly image of one who as God-forsaken and damned overcomes hell through his almighty love and so witnesses that he is God's dearest Son, given to all of us as our own, if only we believe.

Fourteenth, abundantly beyond that, he did not only overcome sin, death, and hell in themselves, offering his victory to our faith; but to offer us more consolation, he suffered the atrocities contained in these three images himself and overcame them.[19] He was assailed and confronted by the images of death, sin, and hell the same way that we are. They made him face the image of death, when the Jewish [authorities] said, "Let him come down from the cross. He helped and healed others. Now he should help himself."[20] As if they were to say, "There, now you face death and you must die. There is nothing that can save you from it." It is the same way that the devil slides the image of death into the view of a dying

144

person and shocks the person's fearful nature with the horribly frightful image.

They held the image of sin before his eyes when they said, "He saved others. If he is the Son of God, let him come down from the cross..."[21] as if to say, "His works were all a fraud and full of deception. He is the son of the devil, not God's son. In body and soul, he belongs to the devil. He never did any good, but only sheer wickedness." They place this devastating image before him until everything seems to have been in vain. And just like the Jewish [authorities] pressed these three images upon Christ to wield confusion, so a person is assailed by all three at the same time in disarray to bewilder and finally drive that one to despair. It is like the way the Lord describes the destruction of Jerusalem in Luke,[22] the enemy surrounds the city with such armed force that there is no escape (that is, death). They squirm in anxiety on all sides, so that they do not know which way to turn (that is, sin). Thirdly, they strike them down to the ground, letting no stone stand upon the other (that is, hell and despair).

They force him to see that devastating image when they say, "He trusted God. Let's see if God hears him and delivers him. He says that he is God's Son."[23] As if to say, "He belongs in hell. God did not elect him. He is damned to eternity. No trusting and no hope will help him, everything was for nothing."

What we see is how Jesus remains completely silent to all these words and gruesome images. He does not argue with them, but acts as if he does not hear and see them. He answers none of them and if he had answered them, he would have only given them cause for even more horrendous raving and ranting. Christ, however, paid attention only to the dear will of his heavenly Father, and that so completely, that he forgets the death, sin, and hell forced upon him and intercedes for them,[24] for their death, sin, and hell. That is the same way that we should dismiss and let drop away the same images—as they wish or will—and have our only thought and consideration be that we cling to the will of God, which is that we attach ourselves to Christ and firmly believe that our death, sin, and hell are overcome in him and they cannot harm us. In this way, the image of Christ remains in us alone, and we dispute and deal with him alone.

Fifteenth, now we arrive at the holy sacraments and their virtues once again to learn the good they do and for what we use them. Those who are permitted the time and grace to receive communion, confession, absolution, and extreme unction (last rites) have a great reason to love, thank, and praise God and die rejoicing. When, in addition, the dying one relies trustingly on the sacrament and believes in it, as mentioned above,[25] then in the sacrament, your God, Christ, who is God's very self deals, speaks, and works with you, through the priest, and what happens there is not human words and work. There, God's very self speaks to you about all things, which we even now said about Christ and how the sacraments are true tokens and documents of how Christ took upon himself and overcame your death by his life; your sin, by his obedience; your hell, by his love. Through the same sacrament, in addition, you become embodied and united with all the saints and enter the veritable communion of the saints, so that they die in Christ with you, bear your sin, and overcome hell. It follows that the sacrament, that is, the external Word of God[26] spoken by the priest, is a great comfort and at the same time a visible sign of divine intention, to which one should hold onto with a staunch faith, like leaning on the goodly staff through which the Patriarch Jacob crossed the Jordan,[27] or like having a lantern by which one is guided to carefully walk with open eyes through the dark passageway of death, sin, and hell. As the prophet says,

"Thy Word, Lord, is a lamp unto my feet and a light unto my path."[28] And St. Peter: "We have a sure Word of God and you will do well to attend to it [like a lamp shining in a dark place]."[29] There is nothing else that can help during the throes of death than this sign, through which all will be saved who will be saved. It points to Christ and his image, which you can oppose against the images of death, sin, and hell. God has addressed me and given me a certain sign of divine grace in this sacrament that the life of Christ has overcome my death in his death; his obedience erased my sin by his suffering; his love has destroyed my hell in his forsakenness. The sign, the promise of my salvation, will not lie to me or deceive me. God said it and God does not lie, not with words or works; and whoever insists in this way and stands on the sacrament will find that his or her election and predestination will turn out well without effort or having to worry.

Sixteenth, now especially this is what it all depends on: that one highly esteem, honor, and entrust oneself to the holy sacrament in which the pure Word of God, the promise, and the sign take place. That means that one does not doubt the sacrament, nor the things of which they are certain signs, for when one doubts, then all is lost—because what happens to us happens according to our belief, as Christ says.[30] What help is it if you imagine death, sin, and hell are overcome in Christ for others, if you do not also believe that your death, your sin, and your hell are overcome and destroyed, and you yourself are thereby saved? Then the sacrament was worthless, because you do not believe the things indicated, given, and promised by the sacrament. That is the vilest sin that can be committed, because you consider God's very self in God's Word, signs, and works to be lying. You see God as someone who says, shows, and promises something that God does not mean or intend to keep. Therefore, we should not joke around with the sacraments. Faith has to attend them and one has to rely on them and cheerfully take the risk with God's signs and promises. What kind of a maker of blessings or God would that be who would not want or wish to save us from death, sin, and hell? What the true God promises and does has to be very great.

So then the devil comes and whispers the thought into your ear, "Oh, what if I have received the sacrament unworthily and by my unworthiness I have thereby robbed myself from receiving such grace?" At this point, sign yourself with the cross and do not allow your worthiness or unworthiness to assault you. Just see to it that you believe that they are certain signs, true words of God, then you are and remain worthy—faith makes you worthy and doubt makes you unworthy. That is why the evil spirit wants to present you with a different kind of worthiness and unworthiness, to induce you to doubt, and with that destroy the sacrament with its works and make God and the Divine Word into a liar. God does not give you anything for the sake of your worthiness. God also does not build the Divine Word and Sacrament upon your worthiness, but upon pure grace. God establishes you, you unworthy one, upon the Divine Word and sign, so hold fast to that and say, "The One who gave me and has given me the divine sign and Word, Christ, life, grace, and heaven, and made my death, sin, and hell unharmful to me, that One is God, who will certainly keep these [promised] things; and if the priest has absolved me, then I can rely on it the way I rely on God's Word itself. If it is God's Word, then it is true and that is my stand, and standing on it I will die." Because you should trust in the priest's absolution so firmly as if God had sent you a special angel or an apostle; yes, even if Christ himself had absolved you.

Seventeenth, the one who receives the sacrament has a veritable advantage, because that one has received God's sign and promise through which one can practice and strengthen one's faith and is called into the image of Christ with these benefits. Others without this sign labor exclusively in faith and receive this sign only by the longing of their hearts. They also thereby receive it, if they stand in the same faith. And this is what you should say concerning the sacrament of the altar. If the priest has given me the holy body of Christ, which is a sign and a promise of communion with all the angels and saints and that they love me and care about me, pray, and suffer with me, die, bear sin, and overcome hell, so it will be and so it must be because the divine sign will not deceive me and I will not allow it to be taken away from me. I would rather deny the whole world along with myself before I would doubt it. My God is certainly truthful and trustworthy for me with the divine signs and promises, whether I am worthy or not. For I am a member of the Christian faith according to the text and declaration of the sacrament. It is better that I be unworthy than that the worthiness of God be placed into question. "Get thee behind me Satan, if you say anything else to me." You see many persons who would gladly like to be certain or would like to have a sign from heaven concerning whether they are right with God and would like to know their predestination. And when such a sign comes over them and they still do not believe it, what help is it to them then? What help are all the signs without faith? What help did the signs of Christ and the apostles provide for the Jews? Even still today, what help is the most holy and worthy sign of the sacrament and Word of God? Why do they not hold with the sacraments, which are the certain and instituted signs that have been tried and tested by all the saints and found to be sure for all those who have faith because they have received what these signs indicate? We should learn to know what they are, for what they serve, and how we should use them. Then, we find that there is not a greater thing on earth that can more lovingly comfort troubled hearts and bad consciences.

For, in the sacraments are God's Words, which serve to show us Christ and the promises against death, sin, and hell, with all the divine possessions, which are God's very self. Now, there is not a lovelier or more desirable thing to hear than that death, sin, and hell are destroyed, which takes place through Christ in us when we use the sacraments rightly. The use is nothing else than having the faith that these things are so, just the way the sacrament promises and pledges through God's Word. Therefore, it is necessary not only to look at the three images in Christ and with these to drive out the opposing images, but also that one has a certain sign that assures us that this has certainly been given to us. That is the function of the sacraments.

Eighteenth, in the hour of death, no Christian person should doubt about not being alone, but be certain that according to the indication of the sacrament, many eyes are watching over one. First of all, those of God's very self, and those of Christ—this because one believes God's Word and cleaves to the sacrament; thereafter, the eyes of the dear angels, the saints, and all Christians. For there is no doubt how the sacrament of the altar shows how all together, as one whole body, they run to the one member to help overcome death, sin, and hell and bear all things with that one. Here, the communion of saints becomes serious and takes place forcefully as a work of love. A Christian person should also take this into consideration and have no doubt about it, and then one can die boldly. Whoever doubts it at that time does not believe in the most holy sacrament of the body of Christ, in which the communion, help, love, comfort, and support of all the saints in all times of need is shown, promised, and pledged. For, if you believe in the signs and the Word of God, then God has an eye on you, the way God says in Psalm 32:8: "I will fix my eyes upon you so that you will not perish." And, if God is watching you, then all the angels are watching over you too, all the saints, and all creatures. Because you remain in the faith, all of them will uphold you in their hands. When your soul leaves, they are there to receive you. You cannot go under. That is shown by the prophet Elisha in Kings, chapter 6, when he spoke to his servant, "Do not be afraid, because there are more with us than with them,"[31] even though the enemy wanted to kill them and no one else was there to see. God, however, opened the eyes of the servant, and he suddenly saw circling them around the mountain a great force of fiery horses and chariots. It is the same for each person who believes in God. Then there is the verse from Psalm 34: "The angel of the Lord shall encamp around those who fear God and deliver them."[32] Those who trust in God shall not be moved, like Mount Zion, which abides forever. High mountains (that is, angels) are surrounding one and God's very self surrounds God's people from now on to eternity. And in Psalm 91:

> For God has charged the angels to bear you up in their hands and guard you wherever you go lest you dash your foot against a stone. You will tread on the lion and the adder, the young lion and the serpent you will trample under foot (that means that all the cunning and treachery of the devil will not be able to harm you), because they trusted in me, I will deliver them; they will be protected because they know my name. When they call upon me I will answer them; I will be with them through all their trials. I will rescue them and honor them. With eternal life, I will satisfy them and show them my salvation.[33]

The apostle similarly says, "The angels, whose numbers are legion, are all ministering spirits and are sent out for the sake of those who are to be saved."[34] Those are all very great things. Who can believe them? Therefore, one must know that God's works are much greater than anyone can imagine and still they work in such a tiny sign of the sacrament in order to teach us what a great thing true faith in God really is.

Nineteenth, no one should presume to do such things through their own strength, but humbly pray to God to create and sustain such a faith and understanding of the divine sacrament. We need to proceed with fear and humility so that we do not ascribe such works to ourselves, but leave God the honor. In addition, the person should call upon the holy angels, especially one's guardian angel, the Mother of God, all the apostles, and especially those saints to whom God gave special devotion. One should also pray in such a way that one not doubt that one's prayer is heard. That for two reasons: the first, was just heard through these Scriptures: how God commanded the angels, as the sacrament provides, that they should give love and help to all those who believe. One should bring that up in prayer and remind them of it. Not that God and the angels do not know it or otherwise would not do it, but so that our faith and trust in them, and through them to God, become ever stronger and more cheerful as we undergo and face death. And second, that God commanded when we pray, that we have a firm faith that what we pray for will take place. And let it be a trusting "Amen." That is why there is a command that we bring this up and remind God of it with prayer. "My God, you have commanded prayer and to believe that my prayer is heard. Because of that I pray and I rely on it, that you will not leave me and you will give me a genuine faith." In addition, for our whole life long, we should pray to God and the saints for a robust faith in the hour of our death, the way we sing so well at Pentecost:

> Now let us pray to the Holy Ghost,
> For true faith of all things the most,

That in our last moments, God may befriend us
and as home we go, God may attend us.[35]

And when the hour has come to die, one should remind God of the same prayer and, besides, of God's commands and promises, without having any doubt that you are heard. For, if God commanded one to pray and to have confidence in prayer and additionally gave us the grace to pray, why should one doubt? God has already done everything so that your prayer is heard and becomes fulfilled.

Twentieth, now look! What more can your God do for you so that you willingly accept death, not fear it, and overcome it? God points to and gives you Christ, who is the image of life, grace, and salvation so that you are not shaken by the images of death, sin, and hell. What is more, God places your death, your sin, your hell on God's dearest Son, overcomes them for you and makes them unharmful to you. In addition, God allows your trials at death with sin, and hell to go over upon the Son and teaches you to be sustained within so that they become harmless and bearable. God gives you all this with a sure and real token, namely, the holy sacrament, so that you never have any doubt. God commands all the divine angels, all the saints, all creatures, that with God's very self they watch over you so that they may preserve, recognize, and receive your soul. God commands that you are to pray for it and be assured that you are heard. What more can or should God do? Therefore, you see that God is a true God, and does right and great godly works on your behalf. Why should not God impose something great upon you (which dying really is) when God provides such advantageous help and strength for it, so that God can test what divine grace can do? As written in Psalm 111: "Great are the works of the Lord; all are selected according to God's pleasure."[36] Because of it, one should pay attention that one gives God's divine will very

153

cheerful and heartfelt thanks for practicing such wonderful, rich, merciful, and immeasurably gracious works for us against death, sin, and hell. So we do not need to fear death quite so much, but rather praise and love God's grace. For love and praise lighten our dying very much, the way God says through Isaiah: [I will bridle your mouth with my praise. I will restrain (my anger) from you, so that I may not cut you off.][37] To that end, may God help us. Amen.

NOTES

FOREWORD

1. "Martin Luther—Witness to Jesus Christ," in *Growth in Agreement* II, ed. J. Gros, H. Meyer, and W. G. Rusch (Grand Rapids, MI: Eerdmans, 2000), 438–42.

2. This is the life's work of A. Herte. Cf. J. Ernesti, "Herte, Adolf," in J. Ernesti and W. Thönissen, *Personenlexikon Ökumene* (Freiburg im Breisgau, 2010), 90f.

3. J. Lortz sets out this hypothesis in *Die Reformation in Deutschland*, vol. 1 (Freiburg im Breisgau, 1940), 176.

4. Homilies and Addresses of Pope John Paul II during his third pastoral visit to Germany (1996) (VApS 126, 32), http://w2.vatican.va/content/john-paul-ii/de/speeches/1996/june/documents/hf_jp-ii_spe_19960622_cathedral-paderborn.html.

5. Apostolic Trip of His Holiness Pope Benedict XVI to Berlin, Erfurt, and Freiburg, September 22–25, 2011 (VApS 189, 71), https://w2.vatican.va/content/benedict-xvi/en/travels/2011/outside/documents/germania.html.

6. *From Conflict to Communion: Lutheran-Catholic Common Commemoration of the Reformation in 2017.* Report of the Lutheran-Roman Catholic Commission on Unity (Leipzig: Evangelische Verlangsanstalt, 2013).

7. "All under One Christ," Roman Catholic/Lutheran Joint Commission Statement on the Augsburg Confession (1980), in *Growth in Agreement*, ed. Harding Meyer and Lukas Vischer (New York/Mahwah, NJ: Paulist Press; Geneva: World Council of Churches, 1984), 241–47.

8. *From Conflict to Communion*, no. 101.

9. Philipp Melanchthon, *Historia de vita et actis Lutheri* (Heidelberg, 1546) (CR 6, 155–70).

PREFACE

1. See Scott Hendrix, "Martin Luther's Reformation of Spirituality," in *Harvesting Martin Luther's Reflections on Theology, Ethics, and The Church*, ed. Timothy J. Wengert (Grand Rapids, MI: William B. Eerdmans, 2004), 240–60.

2. Smalcald Articles, 1, 4 in *The Book of Concord: The Confessions of the Evangelical Lutheran Church*, ed. Robert Kolb and Timothy J. Wengert (Minneapolis: Fortress Press, 2000), 300. The prayer from the Magnificat, *Luther's Works: Word and Sacrament*, ed., Robert H. Fischer, Helmut Lehmann, and Jaroslav Pelikan (Philadelphia: Fortress Press, 1955–1986), 21, 355. Hereafter referred to as LW. Cited in Jeroslav Pelikan, *Mary Through the Centuries: Her Place in the History of Culture* (New Haven: Yale University Press, 1996), 159.

3. See further. In addition, in his morning and evening prayers in the *Small Catechism*, Luther concludes, "Let your holy angel be with me, so that the wicked foe may have no power over me. Amen." See "The Morning and Evening Blessing" in the *Small Catechism* in the *Book of Concord*, 363–64.

4. See further. Also cited in Hans-Werner Scheele, "'A People of Grace,' Ecclesiological Implications of Luther's Sacrament-Related Sermons of 1519," in *Luther's Ecumenical Significance*, ed. Peter Manns and Harding Meyer (Philadelphia: Fortress Press, 1984), 127.

5. See Peter Manns, "The Validity and Theological-Ecumenical Usefulness of the Lortzian Position on the 'Catholic Luther,'" in *Luther's Ecumenical Significance*, 15.

6. Brendt Hamm, *The Early Luther: Stages in a Reformation Reorientation*, trans. Martin J. Lorhmann, Lutheran Quarterly Books (Grand Rapids: Eerdmans, 2014), xi.

7. H. George Anderson et al., ed., *The One Mediator, The Saints, and Mary: Lutherans and Catholics in Dialog VIII* (Minneapolis: Augsburg, 1992).

8. See the forthcoming biography *Martin Luther* by Thomas Kaufmann, trans. Peter Krey in Reformation Resources: 1517–2017, ed. Philip D. Krey and William G. Rusch (Grand Rapids, MI: William B. Eerdmans, 2016). Kaufmann thoroughly discusses Luther's role as heretic. On the other hand, Eero Huovinen quotes Cardinal Jan Willebrand, applying the title of "common doctor" to Luther, while the former Roman Catholic Bishop of Mainz, Karl Lehmann, gives him the title "Teacher of the Faith," for his role in linking his teachings to the tradition. See Eero Huovinen, "Martin Luther: A Common Teacher, *Doctor Communis?* The Ecumenical Significance of Martin Luther," *Seminary Ridge Review* 17, no. 2 (Spring 2015): 23. See also Beth Kreitzer, *Reforming Mary: Changing Images of the Virgin Mary in Lutheran Sermons of the Sixteenth Century* (Oxford: Oxford University Press, 2004), 6–11, in which she discusses the state of the research on the question of Luther's devotion to Mary. She cites William Cole as concluding that "Only a complex answer is possible...." See William Cole, "Was Luther a devotee of Mary?" *Marian Studies* 21 (1970): 94–202.

INTRODUCTION

1. See Joseph Lortz, "Martin Luther: Grundzüge einer geistigen Struktur," in *Reformata Reformanda: Festaufgabe für Hubert Jedin zum 17 Juni 1965*, ed. Erwin Iserloh and Konrad Repgen (Münster: Ashchendorf, 1965), 241. See also Steven Ozment, *The Age of Reform: An Intellectual History of Late Medieval and Reformation Europe* (New Haven: Yale University Press, 1980), 241.

2. See also Lortz, "Martin Luther," 219.

3. Eric Gritsch, "The Views of Luther and Lutheranism on the Veneration of Mary," in *The One Mediator, The Saints, and Mary: Lutherans and Catholics in Dialog VIII*, ed. H. George Anderson, J. Francis Stafford, and Joseph A. Burgess (Minneapolis: Augsburg, 1992), 235–248 at 235.

4. Gritsch, "The Views of Luther and Lutheranism," 235.

5. Walter Tappolet, *Das Marienlob der Reformatoren: Martin Luther, Johannes Calvin, Huldrych Zwingli, Heinrich Bullinger* (Tübingen: Katzman Verlag, 1962), 357–64. Also cited in Gritsch, "The Views of Luther and Lutheranism," 235–37. The *Small and Large Catechisms* that Luther composed in 1528–29 also demonstrate a strong link to and a reform of medieval catholic catechetical spirituality.

6. Gritsch, "The Views of Luther and Lutheranism," 237–38.

7. For an analysis of Marian devotion in the context of the later medieval period, see Beth Kreitzer, "Reforming Mary: Changing Images of the Virgin Mary," in *Lutheran Sermons of the Sixteenth Century* (Oxford: Oxford University Press, 2004), 11–25.

8. Elina Vuola cites Kirsi Sjerna, noting that Luther has a "strong critique of social power" in the Magnificat, in "The Ecumenical Mother Mary and Her Significance for Lutheran Tradition," in *Seminary Ridge Review* 17, no. 2 (Spring 2015): 10. See also Kirsi Stjerna, "For the Sake of the Future: Rekindling Lutheran Theology on Spirituality, Equality, and Inclusivity," in *Lutheran Identity and Political Theology*, Church of Sweden Research Series 9, ed. Carl-Henric Grenholm and Götan Gunner (Eugene, OR: Pickwick, 2014), 83–100.

9. LW 21, 326–27.

10. Pelikan, *Mary Through the Centuries*, 157.

11. Ibid., 157–58. See also the works he cites, Heiko Oberman, *The Virgin Mary in Evangelical Perspective* (Philadelphia: Fortress Press, 1971); and David Wright, *Chosen by God: Mary in Evangelical Perspective* (London: Marshall Pickering, 1989); Arthur Karl Piepkorn, "Mary's Place within the People of God according to Non-Catholics," *Marian Studies* 18 (1967): 46–83.

12. LW 35, 192–93. See also Walter Tappolt and Albert Ebneter, *Das Marienlob der Reformatoren,* (Tübingen: Katzman Verlag, 1962), 20–22. See also Roland H. Bainton, *The Martin Luther Christmas Book* (Philadelphia: Fortress Press, 1948), 21.

13. Gritsch, "The Views of Luther and Lutheranism," 236.

14. Ibid., 236–37.

15. This image of Mary has also been critiqued by feminist theologians for this same reason. See Elina Vuola, "The Ecumenical Mother Mary and Her Significance for Lutheran Tradition," *Seminary Ridge Review* 17, no. 2 (Spring 2015): 11–12.

16. Elina Vuola discusses the resonance between Luther's critique of economic disparity and Liberation Theology, ibid., 11.

17. See pp. 27, 28. See also Philip D. Krey and Peter D. Krey., *Martin Luther's Spirituality*, Classics of Western Spirituality, ed., Bernard McGinn (New York/Mahwah, NJ: Paulist Press, 2005), 95; and also LW 21, 299.

18. Gritsch, "The Views of Luther and Lutheranism," 237.

19. Krey, *Luther's Spirituality*, xv.

20. See Robert Jenson, "An Attempt to Think about Mary," *Dialog: A Journal of Theology* 31 (Fall 1992): 261–62.

21. See also René Laurentin, "Mary's Presence in the Liturgy and Worship of the Church," in *Mary in Scripture, Liturgy, and the Catholic Tradition* (New York/Mahwah, NJ: Paulist Press, 2011), 45–61. Laurentin writes, "The evangelist speaks about her organic role in the Communion of Saints in John 2:12, in which after the first 'sign,' which inspires faith in the disciples, Mary and her family remain with Jesus and his disciples at Capernaum, near Cana. This same reference to the organic place of Mary in the Christian community is explained later in Acts 1:14, where Mary and her family (Jesus' cousins) are assembled with the women to prepare the Feast of Pentecost" (47).

22. George Tavard, "Medieval Piety in Luther's *Commentary on the Magnificat*," in *Ad fontes Lutheri: Toward the Recovery of the Real Luther-Essays in Honor of Kenneth Hagan's Sixty-Fifth Birthday*, ed. Timothy Maschke, Franz Posset, and Joan Skocir (Milwaukee: Marquette University Press, 2001), 281–300. See also Gritsch: "Mary is a model for theologians who need to properly distinguish between human and divine works. She divides all the world into two parts and assigns to each side three works and three classes of persons, so that either side has its exact counterpart to the other. Like Jeremiah (9:23–24), Mary sees wisdom, might, and riches on one side and kindness, justice, and righteousness on the other. The former reflect human works, the latter the works of God. God uses God's

works to down the works of persons, who are always tempted to deify themselves. God's works are 'mercy' (v. 50), 'breaking spiritual pride' (v. 51), 'putting down the mighty' (v. 52), 'exalting the lowly' (v. 53), 'filling the hungry with good things,' and 'sending the rich away empty' (v 53)" ("The Views of Luther and Lutheranism," 237).

23. Tavard, "Medieval Piety in Luther's *Commentary on the Magnificat,*" 281. See also Pelikan, who notes that Luther's Marian devotion is rooted in the role of the creeds—the Trinity in particular—in liturgy and worship (*Mary Through the Centuries,* 157–58). See also René Laurentin, "Mary's Presence in the Liturgy and Worship of the Church," 45–61.

24. Tavard, "Medieval Piety in Luther's *Commentary on the Magnificat,*" 300.

25. Cited in Gritsch, "The Views of Luther and Lutheranism," 237.

26. *Luther's Spirituality,* 151.

27. See Horst Gorski, *Die Niedrigkeit seiner Magd: Darstellung und theologische Analyse der Mariologie Martin Luthers als Beitrag zum gegenwärtigen lüterish/römisch–katholischen Gespräch* (Frankfurt: Peter Lang, 1987), 266.

28. Cited also in Berndt Hamm, *The Early Luther: Stages in a Reformation Reorientation, Lutheran Quarterly Books* 9 (Grand Rapids, MI: Eerdmans, 2014), 148. LW 42, 113.

29. Hamm, *The Early Luther,* 148–49. Hamm shows how Luther extends the notion of intercession from living saints who are to intercede for one another to those who are in heaven.

30. Hamm, *The Early Luther,* 149.

31. See p. 84.

32. See Robert Jenson, *Visible Words: The Interpretation and Practice of Christian Sacraments* (Philadelphia: Fortress Press, 1978), 181ff.

33. See p. 88.

34. See p. 91.

35. See p. 92.

36. See p. 91.

37. See "That These Words of Christ, 'This is my body,' etc., Still Stand Firm against the Fanatics," LW 37:3, ed., Robert H. Fischer, Helmut Lehmann, and Jaroslav Pelikan (Philadelphia: Fortress Press, 1955–1986), 7. For Luther "flesh" in the Hebrew sense does not refer to physicality, but to the body or mind oriented away from God and neighbor.

38. "That These Words of Christ, 'This is my body,'"etc., (1527 LW 37:72). Cited in Oswald Bayer, *Theology The Lutheran Way*, ed. and trans. Jeffrey G. Silcock and Mark C. Mattes, Lutheran Quarterly Books (Grand Rapids: William B. Eerdmans, 2007), 46.

39. Bayer, *Theology The Lutheran Way*, 47.

40. Ibid., 48.

41. Krey, *Luther's Spirituality*, 63.

42. Rom 12:5; 1 Cor 12:5.

43. See p. 109.

44. Pelikan, *Mary Through the Centuries*, 11.

45. See Jenson, *Visible Words*, 181ff.

46. Berndt Hamm explains, "By referring to the generous *communio sanctorum* that he so clearly stressed at the sermon's end, Luther did not mean the people around the deathbed but heavenly 'benevolent powers.' For since no one can come to faith by his or her own strength but rather, God creates and sustains it in the soul, being ready means nothing other than to 'implore God and his dear saints our whole life long for true faith in the last hour, as we sing so fittingly on the day of Pentecost'" (*The Early Luther*, 152).

47. Hamm comments, "The traditional notion of a battle of otherworldly powers at the deathbed was certainly theologically sharpened and surpassed; it remains characteristic of Luther's theology that a sinner's location between law and gospel means that the relationship to death is stamped by a lifelong conflict between fear and comfort. But it was already clear in 1519 that faith was the only way to prepare for dying and that one became certain of salvation by trusting God's victory over death, sin, and hell." (*The Early Luther*, 151).

48. Berndt Hamm notes, "In good medieval fashion, Luther integrated the visualization of the entire *communio sanctorum* into the sacramentally given presence of God and Christ to the dying

(especially at the end of his sermon in paragraphs 18 and 19). If the body of Christ is given to the dying through the Lord's Supper, then this is a sign, promise and assurance to faith that they are accompanied by the protective aid and defense of the community of all the angels, saints, and Christians." (*The Early Luther*, 148).

49. Hamm, *The Early Luther*, 148.

THE MAGNIFICAT PUT INTO GERMAN AND EXPLAINED

1. John Frederick (1503–54), the nephew of Frederick the Wise, succeeded his uncle and became Elector of Saxony in 1532. Beginning in the Fall of 1520, he was in correspondence with Luther, whom he called his "spiritual father" (WA Br 2, 237, 2; 238, 17).

2. See Tavard, "Medieval Piety in Luther's *Commentary on the Magnificat*," 300: "The Virgin Mary and her song of thanksgiving stand as models of true *pietas*, a word which, in its original sense that was still operative at the end of the Middle Ages, designated the mutual affection between parents and children. The praise of Mary is part of the Christian joy."

3. Tavard, "Medieval Piety in Luther's *Commentary on the Magnificat*," 292–96.

4. Luther and others frequently identified themselves this way in their correspondence with the princes.

5. Prov 21:1.

6. See also 2 Sam 14:17; 19:27.

7. See "Commentary on Psalm 82" in Krey, *Luther's Spirituality*, 19.

8. Luther made frequent references to Bias, a Greek sage (ca. 620–540 BC).

9. The Magnificat was regularly sung during Vespers/Evening Prayer and still has a prominent place in both the Roman Catholic and Lutheran liturgies of Evening Prayer.

10. *Er habs denn on mittel von de(m) heyligen geyst.*

11. Cf. 1 Sam 2:6–8; Job 22:29; Ps 75:8; Ezek 21:31; Matt 23:12; Luke 14:11; 18:14.

12. The American edition notes, "An apparent allusion to the old axiom, *Ex nihilo nihil fit.*"

13. *Du sitzest über de(n) Cherubin/und sihest ynn die tieffe oder abgrund.* The NRSV includes this in the apocryphal additions to Daniel, verse 32.

14. *Caro, anima, spiritus.*

15. Exod 26; 36:3–38; 40:1–16.

16. *vorstandt.*

17. *wissen.*

18. *erkentnisz.*

19. Vulgate 67, 7.

20. For a full discussion with a comprehensive bibliography of the influence of monasticism on Luther, especially the spirituality of the Augustinian Order, and Luther's reluctant break with monastic vows, see Heiko A. Oberman, "Luther Contra Medieval Monasticism: Friar in the Lion's Den," in *Ad fontes Lutheri*, 183–213.

21. The treatise "On Good Works" of 1520 appears in WA 6, 204, 13–209, 23. See also WA 9 (226) 229–301. Concerning faith as the greatest work, see WA 6, 204, 13–209, 23. As a work fulfilling the first commandment, see WA 6, 209, 24–216, 11.

22. *Mein seel macht yhn grosz das ist mein gantzes leben weben synn und kraft halten viel von yhm alszo das sie gleich ynn yhn vorzuckt und empor erhebung fuelet ynn seinen gnedigen gutten willenn wie der volgend versz weyszet* (Luke 1:47).

23. Ps 49:18. NRSV says, "For you are praised when you do well for yourself."

24. Compare to Bernard's four stages of love. See "On Loving God," in *Bernard of Clairvaux: Selected Works*, trans. G. R. Evans, Classics of Western Spirituality (New York/Mahwah, NJ: Paulist Press, 1987), 192–97. See also, "Sermon 83," in *Bernard of Clairvaux: On The Song of Songs IV* (Kalamazoo, MI: Cistercian Publications, 1980), 180–87.

25. The RSV has a different rendering of this passage, "Though in their lifetime they count themselves happy—for you are praised when you do well for yourself."

26. See p. 43.

27. Matt 18:9.

28. Augustine, *Confessions*, Book Eight, Chapter 8.

29. Ps 4:6; Ps 27:9; Ps 31:16.

30. See Vuola: "By and large, it can be said that Luther's relationship to the Virgin Mary is positive, even warm and affectionate. There is a Marian spirituality and importance given to Mary in Luther's thinking." ("The Ecumenical Mother," 10).

31. See Eph 1:11 and 1:23.

32. Following a medieval pattern, Luther considers these six works in order. We have omitted this lengthy section from this volume. See SA; LW 21, 332–55. See George Tavard, "Medieval Piety in Luther's *Commentary on the Magnificat*," 281–300 for an analysis of this medieval genre.

SERMON AT COBURG

1. The original text is in German. See LW 51, 197.

2. See p. 72.

3. See Phil 3 and Rom 12.

4. "Christopher is derived from the Greek contraction of the name of Christ (*Christos*) and the verb *pherein* (to bear)." LW 51, 202n1.

5. *Evangelisch*, a gospel believer.

THE SACRAMENT OF PENANCE

1. Ed. note: The abbreviation stands for Luther, Augustinian at Wittenberg. Having become a novice in this most rigorous order in Erfurt, Luther was a member of the Augustinian order there at the time and continued to wear his cowl until 1524.

2. Following confession, the priest assigned certain good works to be done as "penances" by way of making satisfaction for sin.

3. Santiago de Compostela.

4. Luther will not list penance as a sacrament shortly thereafter, but the Lutheran Confessions list penance as a sacrament. See "The Number and Use of the Sacraments," in *The Apology to the Augsburg Confession, The Book of Concord: The Confessions of the Evan-*

gelical Lutheran Church, ed. Robert Kolb and Timothy J. Wengert (Minneapolis: Fortress Press, 2000), 219: "Therefore the sacraments are actually baptism, the Lord's Supper, and absolution (the sacrament of repentance [penance]). For these rites have the command of God and the promise of grace, which is the essence of the New Testament."

5. *Anfechtung* means "spiritual trial."

6. Matt 8:13; 9:29.

7. Augustine, Tract 80, 3, *Tractates On the Gospel of John, 55–111, The Fathers of the Church* 4, trans. John W. Rettig (Washington, DC: Catholic University of America Press, 1988). See also CC 36:529.

8. The sin against the Holy Spirit (Matt 12:22–32) is thus unbelief. Later, Luther will also associate the sin of unbelief with "original sin."

9. See Martin Luther, The *Keys* (1530) in LW 40, 338–45.

10. The Vulgate 85:15 and NRSV 86:15.

11. Isa 40:1, 9 (Vulgate).

12. See paragraph no. 6 above, p. 78.

13. Ed. note: The manuals of penance included catalogs of sins with a penance assigned for each sin.

14. Where Luther provides the Psalm reference to the Vulgate version, in which Psalms 1—146 are numbered differently than the NRSV, we have given the NRSV number.

15. See p. 88.

THE HOLY AND BLESSED SACRAMENT OF BAPTISM

1. Ed. note: Having become a novice in this most rigorous order in Erfurt, Luther was a member of the Augustinian order there at the time and continued to wear his cowl until 1524.

2. Ed note: Luther argues here for the practice of full immersion in the baptismal rite, which was the practice of the early church and the Latin church until the twelfth century.

3. "Lifted out of the baptismal water."

4. 2 Pet 2:5; 1 Pet 3:20–21.

5. Ed. note: Luther often cited scripture from memory and thus his citations vary from current versions.

6. "The Blessed Sacrament of the Holy and True Body of Christ and the Brotherhoods (1519), which is included in this volume. See pp. 106–24.

7. Augustine of Hippo, "Marriage and Desire" (419/420), Book 1, 25, 28. *Answer to Pelagians II,* trans Roland J. Taske, SJ, The Works of Augustine: A Translation for the 21st Century (New York: New City Press, 1998), 46. See also "On Marriage and Concupiscence," *St. Augustine Anti-Pelagian Writings,* Nicene and Post Nicene Fathers, ed. Philip Schaff (New York: The Christian Literature Company, 1887), 5:274; See also CSEL 42,240.

8. 1 Pet 2:10; Luke 2:14; Eph 5:1.

9. See "The Sacrament of Penance" in this volume pp. 76–89.

THE BLESSED SACRAMENT OF THE HOLY AND TRUE BODY OF CHRIST, AND THE BROTHERHOODS

1. Saint Augustine, *Homilies on the Gospel of John 1–40,* trans. Edmund Hill, OP, The Works of Saint Augustine: A Translation for the 21st Century (New York: New City Press, 2000), 439 (25:12). See also CCL 36,254.

2. Rom 12:5; 1 Cor 12:5.

3. Isa 60:14; Heb 12:22; Rev 3:12.

4. See *Sermon on the Ban,* LW 39, 7–22.

5. 1 Cor 11:24–25.

6. See St. Augustine's commentary on Psalm 22:26 (Vulgate 21:27) in *St. Augustine on the Psalms,* trans Dame Scholastica Hughes and Dame Felicitas Corrigan, Ancient Christian Writers (New York/Mahwah, NJ: Paulist Press, 1960), 1:221.

7. 1 Cor 11:21, 33; Acts 2:44–46.

8. In this treatise and elsewhere, Luther is more concerned with the presence of Christ in the elements than he is in the controversy over how Christ is present. See *Confession Concerning Christ's*

Supper: "Now I have taught in the past [In the *Babylonian Captivity* (LW 36, 287)] and still teach that this controversy is unnecessary, and that it is of no great consequence whether the bread remains or not. I maintain, however, with Wycliffe that the bread remains, on the other hand, I also maintain with the sophists that the body of Christ is present" (LW 37, 296).

9. See *The Sacrament of Penance*, pp. 76–89.

10. *Opus operatum* is an action that is done, completed, finished, considered as such without reference to the doer [the administrant] of it. The efficacy of the sacrament, therefore, depends upon the valid performance of the sacrament itself and does not depend upon the sanctity of the minister performing the sacrament.

11. *Opus operantis* is an action considered with reference to the doer of it, the action and holiness of the one acting.

12. 1 Cor 11:30.

THE CONFESSION CONCERNING CHRIST'S SUPPER

1. Meaning in this case the Occamist Scholastics, from whom Luther adapted this analysis of the modes of existence or presence.

2. *Begreiflich* could also be translated "comprehensible" or "determinate" in the sense of measureable.

3. Matt 28:2; John 20:19.

4. The theory of Alleosis was argued, for example, by the Swiss Reformer Zwingli, who insisted that the divine and the human natures of Christ had to be kept separate so that the divine nature was protected from being thought to suffer; that is, when something was said about the divinity of Christ, which after all belongs to his humanity, or vice versa. See the lengthy discussion in "The Solid Declaration," in the *Book of Concord*, 623–24.

5. Exod 3:5; John 3:3.

6. In the deleted paragraph, Luther notes: "[The humanity of Christ] is one person with God, so that wherever God is, there

also is the man; what God does, the man also is said to do; what the man suffers, God also is said to suffer."

7. John 16:28.

A SERMON ON PREPARING TO DIE

1. Matt 7:14.

2. Commonly spelled *natalis* today, the word refers to a birthday or anniversary.

3. John 16:21.

4. Mark 9:23.

5. Luke 1:38.

6. The German word *Tugend*, contrasted with *Untugend*, can mean virtues versus evils or vices. The German words originally meant "to be useful" or "to be capable of." Thus, what are the sacraments capable of doing? What evils do they overcome?

7. Ps 51:3.

8. "Paint the devil on your door" is a German figure of speech meaning to anticipate negative things; so Luther is exhorting the reader to avoid negative thoughts, thoughts that bring you down.

9. Rev 14:13.

10. John 16:33.

11. Gal 6:2.

12. See Matt 11:28.

13. 1 Cor 15:57.

14. 1 Pet 3:19.

15. Matt 27:46.

16. Gen 12:3.

17. Isa 9:3(4).

18. Isa 9:4.

19. See Heb 4:15, 2:18.

20. See Matt 27:40–42.

21. See Matt 27:42–43.

22. Luke 19:43–44.

23. Matt 27:43.

24. See Luke 23:34.

25. See p. 136.

26. According to Augustine, "The Word reaches the element and makes the sacrament, with the effect that even at that time the Word itself becomes visible." (*Tractatus in Evangelium Joannis* 80:3; MPL 35:1840=CCLL 36:529=Mirbt-Aland No. 382).

27. Gen 32:11 (10).

28. Ps 119:105.

29. 2 Pet 1:19.

30. Matt 8:13; 15:28; 21:21.

31. 2 Kgs 6:16ff.

32. Ps 34:8.

33. Ps 91:11–16. Luther writes, "I will show them my eternal grace."

34. See Heb 1:14.

35. See LW 53, 263–64 for the full text.

36. Ps 111:2.

37. Isa 48:9. Luther's rendition of the verse is closer to the Vulgate. The Jerusalem Bible translates the verse, "For the sake of my name I deferred my anger, for the sake of my honor, I have curbed it. I did not destroy you."

BIBLIOGRAPHY

PRIMARY SOURCES

The Major Sources of Martin Luther's Works cited and their
abbreviations follow:

WA. Luther, Martin. *D. Martin Luthers Werke: Kritische Gesamtausgabe.*
   97 vols. Weimar: Bochlaus Nachfolger, 1883–.
————. *Briefwechsel.* 18 vols. in *D. Martin Luther's Werke: Kritische
   Gesamtausgabe.* Weimar: Bochlaus Nachfolger, 1906–61.
————. *Deutsche Bibel.* 12 vols. in *D. Martin Luther's Werke: Kritische
   Gesamtausgabe.* Weimar: Bochlaus Nachfolger, 1906–61.
————. *Tischreden.* 6 vols. in *D. Martin Luther's Werke: Kritische
   Gesamtausgabe.* Weimar: Bochlaus Nachfolger, 1912–21.
————. *Werke.* 61 vols. in *D. Martin Luther's Werke: Kritische
   Gesamtausgabe.* Weimar: Bochlaus Nachfolger, 1983–.
SA. Luther, Martin. *Studienausgabe.* Edited by Hans-Ulrich Delius,
   6 vols. Berlin: Evangelische Verlaganstalt, 1979–99.
LW. *Luther's Works American Edition.* Edited by Jaroslav Pelikan
   (vols. 1–30) and Helmut T. Lehman (vols. 31–54). 55 vols.
   St. Louis: Concordia Publishing House and Philadelphia:
   Fortress Press, 1955.

SECONDARY SOURCES

Anderson, H. George, J. Francis Stafford, and Joseph A. Burgess, eds. *The One Mediator, The Saints, and Mary,* Lutherans and Catholics in Dialogue VIII. Minneapolis: Augsburg, 1992.

Bainton, Roland H. *The Martin Luther Christmas Book.* Philadelphia: Fortress Press, 1948.

Bayer, Oswald. *Theology the Lutheran Way,* Lutheran Quarterly Books. Translated by Jeffrey G. Silcock and Mark C. Mattes. Grand Rapids: Eerdmans, 2007.

Brown, Raymond E. et al. *Mary in the New Testament.* Philadelphia: Fortress Press, 1978.

Cole, William. "Was Luther a Devotee of Mary?" *Marian Studies* 21 (1970): 94–202.

Gorski, Horst. *Die Niedrigkeit siener Magd: Darstellung und theologische Analyse der Mariologie Martin Luthers als Beitrag zum gegenwärtigen luterish/römisch-katholischen Gespräch.* Frankfurt: Peter Lang, 1987.

Gritsch, Eric W. "The Views of Luther and Lutheranism on the Veneration of Mary." In *The One Mediator, the Saints, and Mary,* Lutherans and Catholics in Dialogue VIII, edited by H. George Anderson et al., 235–48. Minneapolis: Augsburg, 1992.

Hamm, Brendt. *The Early Luther: Stages in a Reformation Reorientation,* Lutheran Quarterly Books. Translated by Martin J. Lohrmann. Grand Rapids: Eerdmans, 2014.

Hendrix, Scott. "Martin Luther's Reformation of Spirituality." In *Harvesting Martin Luther's Reflections on Theology, Ethics, and the Church,* Lutheran Quarterly Books, edited by Timothy J. Wengert, 240–60. Grand Rapids: Eerdmans, 2004.

Jenson, Robert. "An Attempt to Think about Mary." *Dialog: A Journal of Theology* 31 (1992): 259–64.

———. *Visible Words: The Interpretation and Practice of Christian Sacraments.* Philadelphia: Fortress Press, 1978.

Kaufmann, Thomas. *Martin Luther.* Translated by Peter Krey. Grand Rapids: Eerdmans, 2016 [forthcoming].

Bibliography

Kolb, Robert, and Timothy J. Wengert, eds. *The Book of Concord: The Confessions of the Evangelical Lutheran Church.* Minneapolis: Fortress Press, 2000.

Kreitzer, Beth. *Reforming Mary: Changing Images of the Virgin Mary in Lutheran Sermons of the Sixteenth Century.* Oxford: Oxford University Press, 2004.

Krey, Philip D., and Peter D. Krey. *Martin Luther's Spirituality,* Classics of Western Spirituality. New York/Mahwah, NJ: Paulist Press, 2005.

Laurentin, René. *Mary in Scripture, Liturgy, and the Catholic Tradition.* New York/Mahwah, NJ: Paulist Press, 2011.

Lortz, Joseph. "Martin Luther: Grundzüge einer geistigen Struktur." In *Reformata Reformanda: Festgabe für Hubert Jedin zum 17 Juni 1965,* edited by Erwin Iserloh and Konrad Repgen, 214–46. Münster: Ashchendorf, 1965.

Manns, Peter. "The Validity and Theological-Ecumenical Usefulness of the Lortzian Position on the "Catholic Luther." In *Luther's Ecumenical Significance: An Interconfessional Consultation,* edited by Peter Manns and Harding Meyer, 3–25. Philadelphia: Fortress Press and New York/Mahwah, NJ: Paulist Press, 1984.

Oberman, Heiko. "Luther Contra Medieval Monasticism: Friar in the Lion's Den." In *Ad fontes Lutheri. Recovery of the Real Luther: Essays in honor of Henneth Hagen's Sixty-Fifth Birthday,* edited by Timothy Maschke, Franz Posset, and Joan Skocir, 183–213. Milwaukee: Marquette University Press, 2001.

———. *The Virgin Mary in Evangelical Perspective.* Philadelphia: Fortress Press, 1971.

Ozment, Steven. *The Age of Reform: An Intellectual History of Late Medieval and Reformation Europe.* New Haven: Yale University Press, 1980.

Pelikan, Jaroslav. *Mary through the Centuries: Her Place in the History of Culture.* New Haven: Yale University Press, 1996.

Piepkorn, Arthur Karl. "Mary's Place within the People of God according to Non-Catholics," *Marian Studies* 18 (1967): 46–83.

Radano, John A. *Lutheran and Catholic Reconciliation on Justification: A Chronology of the Holy See's Contributions, 1961–1999, to a New Relationship between Lutherans and Catholics and to Steps*

Leading to the Joint Declaration on the Doctrine of Justification. Grand Rapids: Eerdmans, 2009.

Scheele, Hans-Werner. "'A People of Grace': Ecclesiological Implications of Luther's Sacrament-Related Sermons of 1519." In *Luther's Ecumenical Significance: An Interconfessional Consultation*, edited by Peter Manns and Harding Meyer, 123–35. Philadelphia: Fortress Press and New York/Mahwah, NJ: Paulist Press, 1984.

Serug, Jacob. *On the Mother of God.* Translated by Mary Hansbury. Crestwood, NY: St. Vladimir's Seminary Press, 1998.

Tappolet, Walter, and Walter Ebneter. *Das Marienlob der Reformatoren: Martin Luther, Johannes Calvin, Huldrych Zwingli, Heinrich Bullinger.* Tübingen: Katzman Verlag, 1962.

Tavard, George. "Medieval Piety in Luther's *Commentary on the Magnificat.*" In *Ad fontes Lutheri: Toward the Recovery of the Real Luther-Essays in Honor of Kenneth Hagan's Sixty-Fifth Birthday*, edited by Timothy Maschke, Franz Posset, and Joan Skocir, 281–300. Milwaukee: Marquette University Press, 2001.

Vuola, Elina. "The Ecumenical Mother Mary and Her Significance for Lutheran Tradition." *Seminary Ridge Review* 17, no. 2 (2015): 1–21.

Wright, David. *Chosen by God: Mary in Evangelical Perspective.* London: Marshall Pickering, 1989.

Wright, Wendy M. *Mary in the Catholic Imagination: Le Point Vierge.* New York/Mahwah, NJ: Paulist Press, 2010.

INDEX

Abel, 50

Absolution, 12–13, 78, 80–84, 86, 88, 99, 148. *See also* Forgiveness

Adam, 44

Ahasuerus, great feast of King, 118

Anne, St., 2

Apostles' Creed, 2, 56–57

Ark, 123

Augsburg Confession, 10, 13

Augustine, St., 78, 96, 107, 113

Authority of Church, 77, 84

Barnabas, 48

Bayer, Oswald, 15

Bias (sage), 25

Bible. *See* Scriptures

Birth of infant, 90–91, 136

Boasting, 40–41, 46, 59, 61, 66

Body. *See* Flesh

Bread. *See under* Sacrament of the Lord's Supper

Cain, 50

Cardinals, tale of two, 49–50

Chastity vow, 102–3

Christ. *See* Jesus

Christians: death and fellowship of, 150–52; faith of, 32–36, 69–71; Sacrament of the Lord's Supper and community of, 17; in Scriptures, 41, 98; suffering of, 9, 67–70, 73–74

Christology of Luther, 18–19

Christopher, St., 9–10, 63, 68–69

Collection, 114

Commandment, First, 60

Communion. *See* Sacrament of the Lord's Supper

Communion of saints, 9–12, 150

Confession, 13, 19, 82, 85–88, 93, 136–37. *See also* Sacrament of Penance

Confession Concerning Christ's Supper, The: Christology of Luther and, 18–19; faith and, 125, 131–32;

grounds for, 125; Jesus'
body and, 126–29, 132–34;
Jesus as God and human
and, 129–32; modes of
object existing in a place
and, 125–28, 133
Contrition, 12–13, 78–79,
82–83, 85–87. *See also*
Confession; Sacrament of
Penance
Council of Ephesus, 23
Cross of Jesus, 15, 24, 65, 73–75.
See also Suffering
"Cross and Suffering." *See*
Sermon at Coburg

Daniel, 6, 27
David, 30–32, 37, 43, 69–70, 83,
89, 110
Death: accepting, 153–54;
birth of infant and, 136;
Christian fellowship and,
150–52; evils of, 137–38,
144–46, 150; fear of,
20, 35, 101, 110, 153–54,
161n47; flesh and, 101;
God and, 29, 135–36;
image of, frightening,
137–38, 144–46, 150;
Luther and, 20–22; *Natale*
and, 20, 136; Sacrament
of the Lord's Supper and,
121–23; sins and, 20–21,
138–39; soul and, 20,
92, 135, 139, 145, 151, 153.
See also "A Sermon on
Preparing to Die"

Definition of Chalcedon, 19
Devil: faith and, attack on,
99–100; God's protection
from, 72–73; Paul and,
72–73; Sacrament of the
Lord's Supper and, 112,
147–48; sins and, 138;
Word of God and, 70–71;
worthiness of self and,
148
Disciples, 112–13, 118, 122, 126.
See also specific name

Elisha, 151
Elizabeth, 7
Estates in life, 101
Esther, Queen, 44
Eucharist. *See* Sacrament of the
Lord's Supper
Eve, 44
Evils: cross of Jesus and, 73; of
death, 137–38, 144–46,
150; in world, 110. *See also*
Devil
Excommunication, 108

Faith: absolution and, 12; of
Christians, 32–36, 69–71;
*The Confession Concerning
Christ's Supper* and, 125,
131–32; devil's attack on,
99–100; Luther and, 18,
21–22; Paul and, 96; in
Sacrament of Baptism, 18,
97–100; in Sacrament of
the Lord's Supper, 18, 21,
106, 117–24; in Sacrament

of Penance, 18, 78, 84–86;
suffering and, 69–71;
weight of, 69–71
False humility, 43–44
False teachers and teachings,
33–34
Fanatics' suffering, 65–66
Fasting, 101–2
Fear: of death, 20, 35, 101, 110,
153–54, 161n47; of God,
25–26, 59–60, 76, 151; of
Jesus, 119; of princes and
rulers, 23, 25; of world,
114, 118
Fellowship, 111, 113–15, 124. *See
also* Sacrament of the
Lord's Supper
Flesh: death and, 101; of Jesus,
14; Mary as Word made, 8;
peace and, 70; Sacrament
of the Lord's Supper and,
114–18; sinful birth of,
90–94, 96, 109, 112; sins
in, 14; soul and, 130; spirit
and, 14–15, 32
Forgiveness: of guilt, 76–79,
85–86, 89; of punishment,
76; in Sacrament of
Baptism, 100; of sins,
76–78, 88–89, 100
Freedom and Jesus, 63–64

Gabriel (angel), 4–5
Geschlechter, 59–60
Gideon, 143–44
God: as Almighty, 27–28; as
Creator, 27; credit to, by

Mary, 37–38, 53–59; death
and, 29, 135–36; devil
and, protecting people
from, 72–73; estates in
life and, 101; faithfulness,
67, 70; fame and, 58; fear
of, 25–26, 59–60, 76, 151;
grace of, 52, 53–55, 82,
104–5, 143; great things
done by, 53–59; holiness
of name, 57–59; honoring,
72–73; humanity and,
130; humble and, 45;
Jesus and, 15–16, 29, 57;
judgment of, 96; knowing,
28; knowledge of self and,
142–43; love of, 23, 28–29,
31, 35–37, 39, 41, 46,
48–49, 52–53, 89, 105, 139,
154; Mary as embodiment
of grace of, 2–4, 6, 36;
Mary as Mother of, 4–5,
8–9, 23, 55–56, 58; mercy
of, 59–62, 98; might
and, inclusions under,
61–62; as Mighty One,
53–59; nature of, seeking,
60; parts of world and,
61–62; plan of, 93–94;
pledge to, 95–96, 102–3;
praising works of, 46–50;
praying to, 22, 152–53;
presence of, 4, 15–16, 125;
Sacrament of the Lord's
Supper and, 109–10; soul
and, 26; suffering of
Christians and, 74; as true

God, 153; unchangeability
of, 36; will of, 35; wisdom
and, inclusions under, 61;
Word of, 5, 8, 70–71, 80,
121, 125, 147; works of, 48,
56–57, 60–61, 120
Grace: of God, 52, 53–55, 82,
104–5, 143; in Sacrament
of Penance, 78, 81–84
Gritsch, Eric, 8–9
Guilt. *See under* forgiveness

Hail Mary, 2, 4
Hamm, Berndt, 11–12
Hannah, 5
Hell, 137, 139–40, 144–46
Holy Spirit: communion
of saints and, 10–11;
Magnificat and, 27; Mary
and, 5; Sacrament of the
Lord's Supper and, 16; in
Scriptures, 7; sin against,
81
Humanity, 28, 94–96, 130
Humble, the, 15, 28, 42–43, 45
Humility, 3, 5–6, 28, 40–46, 154

Incarnation, 15
Indulgences, 13, 76–77, 104
Isaiah, 30, 85, 104, 143–44, 154

Jeremiah, 46, 127
Jerusalem, 41
Jesus: behavior on cross, 143–
46; birth of, 30; body of,
126–29, 131–34; cross of,
15, 24, 65, 73–75; death
and, 136; fear of, 119;
flesh of, 14; freedom and,
63–64; God and, 15–16, 29,
57; as God and human,
129–32; going through
water with, 69–70; images
of, 12, 143–44; incarnation
of, 15; Lord's Supper and
body of, 14–15; love of,
17–18, 146–47; Mary as
mother of, 7; Sacrament
of the Lord's Supper and,
17, 111–14, 116, 118, 123;
sacraments and, 136–37;
sins and, 141–42; suffering
of, 9–10, 17, 64–67
John, St., 46, 116
John Frederick of Saxony, 2, 8,
23–26
Judas, 83

Knight, 71–72
Koinonia of saints, 11

Leaders, 23, 25
Lord's Supper, 14–19. *See also*
Sacrament of the Lord's
Supper
Lortz, Joseph, 1
Love: communion of saints
and, 150; fellowship and,
108; of God, 23, 28–29, 31,
35–37, 39, 41, 46, 48–49,
52–53, 89, 105, 139, 154;
of Jesus, 17–18, 146–47;
Sacrament of Baptism
and, 96, 101; Sacrament

of the Lord's Supper and, 108, 111, 115–16, 119–22, 124; of Scriptures, 24

"Low estate," 23, 29, 40–53

Luke, 43

Luther, Martin: baptism and, 13–14; baptismal calling and, 9–10; Christology of, 18–19; communion of saints and, 9–12; death and, 20–22; faith and, 18, 21–22; Hail Mary and, 4; John Frederick of Saxony and, letter to, 24–26; Lord's Supper and, 14–19; Magnificat and piety of, 2; Mary and piety of, 1–10, 23; Ninety-Five Theses and, 12–13; penance and, 12–14; piety of, 1–9, 23; prayer and, 22; predestination and, 21; Sacrament of Baptism and, 13–14; sacraments and, 12–19, 21–22; Scriptures and, interpreting, 21; spiritual and, 14; supernatural and, 11–12; theology of, 1, 13–19; transubstantiation and, 12, 18–19. *See also specific work*

Magnificat: boasting and, 46; commentary on, early, 23–24; editors' introduction to, 23–24;

faith of Christians and, 32–36; God as almighty and, 27–28; God as Creator and, 27; great things done by God and, 53–59; Holy Spirit and, 27; honoring of Mary and, 51–53; humility and, 40–46; introduction of, 5–6; lovers and, impure, 39; "low estate" and, 40–53; Luther's letter to John Frederick of Saxony and, 24–26; Luther's piety and, 2; Mary and, 27–30; mercy of God and, 59–62; moderation and, 40; praising God's works and, 46–50; shoot and stump metaphor and, 30–31; song of praise and, 26–27, 37; soul magnifying God and, 26, 31–38, 61; spirit and, 32–34, 38–40; Tavard's summary of, 7–8; writing of, 23

Mary: as blessed of all women, 7; communion of saints and, 10–11; credit to God by, 37–38, 53–59; as embodiment of God's grace, 2–4, 6, 36; Holy Spirit and, 5; honoring, 51–53; humility of, 40–41; life of, 29–30; low estate of, 23, 29, 40–41, 45, 50–53; Luther's piety and, 1–10, 23; Magnificat and, 27–30; as Mother of God, 4–5, 8–9, 23, 55–56, 58; as mother of Jesus, 7; pregnancy of, 7; as saint, 5; spirit of, 40; as Word made flesh, 8; works of God and, 60–61

Mass, 80, 113–14, 118–20, 122
Matrimony, estate of, 101, 103–4
Melanchthon, Philipp, 10, 13
Merchant, 71
Mercy of God, 59–62, 98
Midianites, attack on, 143–44
Might, God's inclusions under, 61–62
Moderation, 40
Moses, 32–33, 44, 59–60, 131

Natale, 20, 136
Nathan, 89
Nicene Creed, 19
Nicodemus, 130–31
Ninety-Five Theses, 12–13
Noah's flood, 93

"On Translating," 4
Opus operatum, 120–21

Passover, 113
Paul, St.: boasting and, 46; collection and, 114; cross of Jesus and, 65; devil and, 72–73; faith and, 96; fellowship and, 111; grace of God and, 53–54; humility and, 28, 41–42;

leaders and, 23, 25; parts of person and, 31–34; Sacrament of Baptism and, 92, 110; Sacrament of the Lord's Supper and, 17, 108–9, 114–15, 119; slanderers and, 119; suffering of Christians and, 67, 70; suffering of Jesus and, 66–67; wages for labor and, 47; wealth and poverty and, 39; works of God and, 48, 56–57

Peace, 34, 70–71
Pelikan, Jaroslav, 19
Penance, 12–14, 86–87, 89, 99. See also Sacrament of Penance
Person, parts of in Scriptures, 31–34
Peter, St.: the humble and, 28; John and, 46; keys of authority and, 77, 84; in prison, 132; Sacrament of Baptism and, 93; Sacrament of Penance and, 77–78; suffering and, 66–67; Word of God and, 80, 89, 147
Pietas, 8
Potter, 93, 103
Poverty, 27, 30, 38–39, 53
Prayer, 22, 152–53
Prayer Book of 1522, 2
Predestination, 21
Punishment, forgiveness of, 76

Purity, 93–94, 97

"*Regina coeli laetare*" (hymn), 55–56

Repentance, 12, 102. *See also* Sacrament of Penance

Riches, 25, 28, 40, 53, 61–62, 71. *See also* Wealth

Sacrament of Baptism: Augustine and, 107; chastity vow and, 102–3; components of, 14; faith in, 18, 97–100; fasting and, 101–2; foreshadowing in Noah's flood and, 93; forgiveness in, 100; function of, 123; God's plan and, 93–94; grace of God and, 104–5; helpfulness to humanity and, 94–96; judgment of God and, 96; life as a spiritual baptism and, 92; love and, 96, 101; Luther's endorsement of, 13–14; Luther's theology and, 13–14; mercy of God and, 98; as one-time ritual, 17; Paul and, 92, 110; Peter and, 93; pledge to God and, 95–96, 102–3; purity and, 93–94, 97; Sacrament of Penance and, 99; satisfaction and, 98–99, 102; significance of, 90–91; as sign or token, external, 91;

sinlessness and, 93–94, 97; sins and, 94–100; suffering and, 100–101, 103–4; *Taufe* and, 90; vow of, 102–3; water in, 92–93

Sacrament of the Lord's Supper: abuses of, 121; adversity assailing people and, 109–10; blessing of, 124; bread in, 106–7, 116–17; collection and, 114; community of Christians and, 17; components of, 16, 106; cruciform living, 9–10; death and, 121–23; devil and, 112, 147–48; disciples and, 112–13; faith in, 18, 21, 106, 117–24; fellowship and, 17, 111, 114–15, 124; flesh of Christ and, 114–18; frequency of, 17; function of, 123–24; God and, 109–10; Holy Spirit and, 16; Jesus and, 17, 111–14, 116, 118, 123; love and, 108, 111, 115–16, 119–22, 124; Luther's theology and, 14–19; Mass and, 113–14, 120, 122; misfortunes of fellowship and, sharing, 111, 114–15; as *opus operatum*, 120–21; in past, 114; Paul and, 17, 108–10, 114–15, 119; reception of, frequency of, 112; sermon on, 13–14; as sign, external, 16, 106–7, 115, 117, 122–23; significance of, 16–17, 106–9, 115–16; sins and, 110–11; slanderers and, 119; soul and, 121, 130; spiritual body and, 119–20; true fellowship and, 114–15; union and, 116; wine in, 106–7, 116–17

Sacrament of Penance: absolution and, 78, 80–83; authority of Church and, 84; books on, lack of, 87; comfort and, 85; confession and, 85, 87–88; contrition and, 87; faith in, 18, 78, 84–86; forgiveness of guilt and, 76–80, 85–86, 89; forgiveness of punishment and, 76; forgiveness of sin and, 76–78, 88–89; grace in, 78, 81–84; indulgences and, 76–77; Luther's protest against, 13; Luther's theology of, 12–14; parts of, 12, 86; penance versus, 86–87; Peter and, 77–78; Sacrament of Baptism and, 99; satisfaction and, 87–88; venial sins and, 87–88

Sacraments: Jesus and, 136–37; Luther and, 12–19, 21–22; "A Sermon on Preparing to Die," and, 137, 146–50. *See also specific rite*

Saints: communion of, 9–12, 150; suffering of, 95. *See also specific saint*

Satan, 149. *See also* Devil

Satisfaction, 12–13, 45, 76–77, 79, 82, 85, 87–88, 98–99, 102, 105

Scriptures: Christians in, 41, 98; comfort from, 71; Holy Spirit in, 7; humility in, 41; Jerusalem in, 41; Jesus' body and, 128; love of, 24; Luther's interpretation of, 21; person in, 31–34; princes in, 25, 28; soul in, 32

Sermon at Coburg: comfort of Scriptures and, 71; communion of saints and, 9–10; cross and, 65–66; devil and, God's protection from, 72–73; editors' introduction to, 63–64; faith of Christians and, 69–71; fanatics' suffering and, 65–66; honoring God and, 72–73; learning from cross and, 74–75; occasion of, 63; overview, 9–10; promises in relation to suffering and, 68; suffering of Christians and, 67–69, 73–74; suffering of Jesus

and, 64–67; weight of
faith and, 69–71

"Sermon on Preparing to Die,
A": accepting death and,
153–54; behavior of Jesus
on cross and, 144–46;
communion of saints
and, 150; confession and,
136–37; evils facing dying
and, 137–40; feeling alone
and, no need for, 150–52;
God and, orienting
toward, 135–36; hell and,
139–40; image of Jesus
and, glowing, 143–44;
Jesus and, gazing at, 142–
43; material possessions
and, arranging before
dying, 135; others who
have died in God's grace
and, considering, 140–41;
overview, 20–22; prayer
to God and, 152–53;
sacraments and, 137, 146–
50; sins and, 138–39, 141–
42; spiritual preparation
and, 135; supernatural
and, 11–12; turning away
from evil images, 140

Shoot and stump metaphor,
30–31

Sinlessness, 93–94, 97

Sins: contrition over, 78; death
and, 20–21, 138–39; devil
and, 138; in flesh, 14;
forgiveness of, 76–78,
88–89, 100; against Holy

Spirit, 81; Jesus and, 141–
42; Sacrament of Baptism
and, 94–100; Sacrament
of the Lord's Supper and,
110–11; "A Sermon on
Preparing to Die" and,
138–39, 141–42; striving
against, 96–97, 100; venial,
87–88

Solomon, 30

Soul: death and, 20, 92, 135,
139, 145, 151, 153; flesh
and, 130; health of, 15;
magnifying God, 26,
31–38, 61; Sacrament of
the Lord's Supper and,
121, 130

Spirit: false, 36–37; false
teachers and, 33; in
Magnificat, 32–34, 38–40,
61

Spiritual, 14

Strohl, Jane, 13

Suffering: of Christians, 9,
67–70, 73–74; cross and,
64–75; faith and, 69–71;
of fanatics, 65–66; of
Jesus, 9–10, 17, 64–67;
Peter and, 66–67;
promises in relation to,
68; Sacrament of Baptism
and, 100–101, 103–4; of
saints, 95

Supernatural, 11–12, 129

Tappolet, Walter, 2

Tavard, George H., 7–8, 24

Transubstantiation, 12,
    18–19
Trinity, 11, 15

Union, 116

Venial sins, 87–88

Water, baptismal, 92–93
Wealth, 30, 38–39, 61. *See also*
    Riches

Wengert, Timothy, 6–7
Wickedness. *See* Evils
Will of God, 35
Wisdom, God's inclusions
    under, 61
Word of God, 5, 8, 70–71, 80,
    89, 121, 125, 147
World, parts of, 61–62
Worthiness of self, 148

Zechariah, 5

P. Krey - Mercer 5/4/17

Despite Ecum. advances, we live in parallel
communities. (even in full communion?)

Cardinal Willebrands - Luther is now a
"common doctor" (like TA)

There is no "virtual" or "spiritual" unity;
must be visible.

Ref (unintended!) happened because the
Church could not "receive" Luther's
reform.